Southwest Museum exhibition dates:
July 13—September 15, 1984

Native Faces: Indian Cultures in American Art

From the Collections of the Los Angeles Athletic Club
and the Southwest Museum

Patricia Trenton and Patrick Houlihan

LAACO Incorporated and the Southwest Museum

To our spouses, whose patience and
loving support made this project possible

Published by LAACO Incorporated
(The Los Angeles Athletic Club)
and the Southwest Museum
Los Angeles, California

Library of Congress Catalog Card Number 84-081186
ISBN 0-916561-00-3

Contents

Directors and Trustees vi

Foreword, Frank G. Hathaway vii

Foreword, Norman F. Sprague, Jr. ix

Preface, Patricia Trenton and Patrick T. Houlihan x

Acknowledgments xii

California

    The California Culture Area 2

    Henry Raschen 5

    Grace Hudson 7

    Pomo Culture in the Raschen and Hudson 11

Southwest

    The Southwest 18

    Hopi Pueblo 20

    William Leigh 23

    Taos Pueblo 29

    Joseph Sharp 33

    Ernest Blumenschein 45

    Oscar Berninghaus 55

    Walter Ufer 63

    Victor Higgins 69

    Kenneth Adams 75

    E. Irving Couse 79

Plains

    The Plains 86

    Joseph Sharp 89

    Edgar Paxson 93

    Warren Rollins 99

    John Hauser 105

Notes 108

Collections and Exhibitions 114

Directors and Trustees

Foreword

The Los Angeles Athletic Club is very pleased to collaborate with the Southwest Museum in the creation of the exhibition *Native Faces* by lending paintings from the club's collection and by funding the exhibition catalog.

Perhaps a few words of history will help the reader to understand how this exhibition came to be and why we find it such an exciting project. The Los Angeles Athletic Club was founded in 1880. Forty-one young men banded together to establish a gymnasium and meeting rooms because of their desire for camaraderie and sports in a wholesome environment. Tiring of rented quarters by 1906, they made plans for a large clubhouse, and in 1912 the monumental building at Seventh and Olive in downtown Los Angeles was dedicated. Today it is designated a cultural monument; at that time the walls were spartan. Although designed with splendid athletic facilities, the club needed furnishings and works of art to match. Officers and committees of the teens and twenties bought sparingly from local artists or dealers. Pictures were also taken in trade for club bills, and by the 1930s art by William Wendt, Benjamin Brown, J. Bond Francisco, Paul Connor, and others of the Plein Air School (less politely called the Eucalyptus School) was predominant. Augmenting those placid landscapes were naval watercolors by Arthur Beaumont and seascapes by Duncan Gleason. A lifesize French nude, *The Awakening of Psyche* by Guillaume Seignac, hung in the men's bar, where it was covered or draped on ladies' nights. So much for history!

In 1964, wanting to go beyond what had become a concentration on landscape, the Board of Directors at my request (I was then club president) authorized a project to buy one or more mainstream Western American pictures that would further enliven the club's surroundings. The search was on, the pulse quickened, the terminal disease that infects any compulsive collector was caught—and away we went.

The first picture was Albert Bierstadt's nocturne with spear fisherman on Lake Tahoe. Thanks to dealer Terry DeLapp and club interior designer Rex Davis, we started with this magnificent work. Staying with the western scene, Ernest Narjot's *Gold Rush Camp*, William Hahn's *Return from the Hunt*, and others were added. In 1966, Dr. Carl Dentzel, late director of the Southwest Museum, offered to advise and assist in our quest. His knowledge and friendship, until his untimely death in 1980, were of inestimable value.

Although my taste, and therefore the club's collection, ran early to Western art, we have also collected American nineteenth-century genre, and twentieth-century social realism. George Luks, J. D. Chalfant, Eugene Speicher, Walt Kuhn, John S. Curry, George Bellows, William Bradford, and many others broaden the collection.

Nevertheless, repeatedly we found that among our best pictures were American Indian subjects, and so the idea came again and again. Why not try to do an exhibition around the faces and persons depicted by these painters of the Indian? Once having decided that this could be a viable theme, we sought additional related pictures—especially those by the Taos Society of Artists. Much credit must be given to three galleries and their owners who have been most important to us in acquisition and research: Gerald Peters of Santa Fe,

Steve Rose of Los Angeles, and Forest Fenn, also of Santa Fe.

What do we look for in a picture? Impact, quality, size, and condition are factors; but to sum up, I believe a picture must have "eye." Some say the buyer or collector must have an eye. Time, history, and the critic will validate or deny the eye responsible for our pictures. If there is any fault, I will assume it. If there is credit, many deserve to share that.

Ideas such as mine are only seeds. Without the support of club officers, particularly the current President Charles Hathaway, the LAACO Board of Directors, the technical and organizational skills of our esteemed new curator, Dr. Patricia Trenton, and the enthusiastic work of the Southwest Museum staff so ably led by Dr. Patrick Houlihan, this exhibition could not have been.

Frank G. Hathaway
Chairman of the Board
LAACO Incorporated

Foreword

Since its founding in 1907 the Southwest Museum has held collections in Western American art. The museum's founder, Charles Lummis, was a contemporary of many Western artists and his home on the Arroyo Seco in Los Angeles a showcase for their art. His house book contains sketches by Edward Borein, Carl Oscar Borg, Gerald Cassidy, Thomas Moran, Frederic Remington, Charles Russell, and others who gathered at his table.

Throughout its history, under directors such as James Scherer, Frederick Hodge, Carl Dentzel, and Patrick Houlihan, the Southwest Museum has advanced knowledge and developed appreciation of the American West and its art. It has done so by broadening the view of Western history and its pictorial record. Today its collections are resources for the study of art of the American West through Indian art and artifacts, Hispanic art and artifacts, painting and sculpture, rare books, maps and documents, and historic photography. All of these resources speak to a view of the American West that encompasses a rich artistic heritage, which the Southwest Museum is pleased to share.

Beyond the resources of its own collections, the museum seeks to present the holdings of other institutions—public and private. This exhibition of paintings from the Los Angeles Athletic Club Collection, with artifacts from the Southwest Museum Collection, seems especially fitting during the summer of 1984 as our city hosts the Olympic Games. It affords an opportunity to present America's native cultures as seen by American artists to Olympic visitors and to the general public of Los Angeles.

California, the Southwest, and the Plains—the three culture areas represented in the paintings and the artifacts chosen for this exhibition—correspond to the sequence of works in the exhibition and catalog. These culture areas also reflect the strengths of the Southwest Museum's collections and permanent installations. It is the diversity of the native cultures in each of these areas—and in one other, the Northwest Coast—that we seek to portray to our visiting public. For both California and the Southwest these collections range in time from the prehistoric through the historic periods, and for all of these culture areas true masterpieces of Indian art are held by the Southwest Museum.

The fact that European and American artists were attracted to the native cultures in these areas and sought to paint them only confirms my belief that artists, as sensitive observers of the world around them, saw a beauty there that they wished to preserve in their art. As I look at these paintings and artifacts, I am cognizant of the unity of the art heritage of the West. It is this continuum of cultural history that enriches our lives and those of our children today. The efforts of the Southwest Museum and the Los Angeles Athletic Club in preserving and presenting this heritage are to be applauded.

On behalf of the Board of Trustees, I would like to thank all who assisted in realizing this project.

Dr. Norman F. Sprague, Jr., President
Board of Trustees
Southwest Museum

Works of art that depict the American Indian are often valuable research documents for both historians and anthropologists. They provide not only an ethnological record of ceremonial rituals, dwellings, camps, and costumes but insight into the white man's perception of native Americans as well.

Long before the period spanned by this exhibition, the American Indian was an object of fascination for artists. His lifeways and all of his colorful trappings contrasted sharply with the restrained mid-Victorian world of the white man and offered fresh and exciting subject matter compared with the "hackneyed European subjects" then in vogue.[1] By the time the frontier was first explored, interest in the new land and its inhabitants was so strong that artists accompanied even the earliest expeditions.

Although many of these early artists attempted to deliver the most realistic depictions possible, they were largely untutored and possessed limited skills. Ironically, as public curiosity about the West grew, the better-trained and more enterprising artists began to produce the more romantic, idealized images demanded by the public. As the potential of the West's natural resources was realized, however, this eighteenth-century view of primitivism faded in favor of harsher economic considerations. The American Indian was increasingly viewed as a social, political, and economic hindrance and thus became expendable. In the native American's losing battle to preserve his heritage and lands, he began to be depicted as a stereotyped composite of bloodthirsty savage and noble warrior accepting his fate.

By the 1840s such artists as George Catlin, Karl Bodmer, and Seth Eastman recognized that the Indian was vulnerable and that his lifeways and lands faced annihilation. These artists began to paint with a different purpose: to record a vanishing culture for posterity. In 1841, Catlin wrote prophetically of both the Indian and the buffalo: "They have fled to the great plains of the West, and there, under an equal doom, they have taken up their *last abode*, where their race will expire, and their bones will bleach together."[2]

The post-Civil War period saw more and more pictorial images of Indians and whites in confrontation. With the extinction of the buffalo and the banishment of Indians to reservations, the race's acculturation was accelerated. Artists, along with most other Americans, felt a great anticipation for the century ahead along with a great nostalgia for the one that was ending. This nostalgia is vividly reflected in the works of Charles Russell, Frederic Remington, and Edgar Paxson, who recognized the implications of technological advances on the already vanishing Indian cultures.

By 1900 the Indian Wars had ended and the transition to reservation life was in progress throughout the Plains. Traditional native subsistence patterns had disappeared with the buffalo herds on which they depended, and the social, political, and religious components of these cultures were under great stress. From its center in Oklahoma, peyote was being diffused to other tribes throughout the West, and in time a pan-Plains culture would be implanted throughout the region.

In the Southwest the railroad was bringing government officials, missionaries, and an ever-growing number of tourists and anthropologists. Among the

Pueblos, Navajos, and Apaches, traditional lifeways were now being observed by whites, and craft objects formerly made for use were now being made for sale. By the turn of the century the Indians of California had suffered considerable disruption, first from their forcible relocation to Spanish missions and later as a result of the Anglo search for gold and other resources on Indian land. Such were the peoples that the artists presented here sought to paint—not the warriors of yesterday, but the survivors of America's "manifest destiny" whose traditional cultures were in a state of transition and would soon disappear.

Eventually, a larger and larger segment of the white population was aroused by the Indian's plight and began to question the merits of acculturation. "Why Americanize the Indian?" asked Mary Austin in a timely and provocative article in *Forum* magazine in 1929. The artists represented in this exhibition asked the same question, albeit usually in a nonpolitical context. Their works, featuring native cultures of California, the Southwest, and the Great Plains, date from 1884 to 1965, although most were painted between 1895 and 1930.

Artists working in the late nineteenth and early twentieth centuries often painted with a sense of urgent mission: to capture this moment of transition, combining the Indian's changing culture with allusions to his past. Some infused their paintings with poignantly romantic visions of the Indian as a heroic, noble savage; others candidly recorded aging Indian leaders before their final journeys to the "shadow hills"; still others blended elements of distinct cultures into a single pictorial idea. All attempted to preserve something of the Indian culture using his own visual language. Each in his unique way contributed to both the creation and the preservation of the myth and reality of the American Indian for future generations.

The paintings in this exhibition embody a wide spectrum of valuable information, from detailed ethnographic observations to the subtle emotional reactions of the artist and his Indian models. Few works of art offer such a rich field of study for both art historian and anthropologist. To emphasize this fact, we have chosen to present this group of paintings from the Los Angeles Athletic Club Collection together with related artifacts from the Southwest Museum Collection in a collaborative exhibition that explores the potential for fruitful interaction between these two disciplines.

It is hoped that students and scholars, armed with a new, more multidimensional viewpoint, will be moved to reexamine the entire body of art devoted to the Indian and his culture. We are certain that a deeper understanding and appreciation of this remarkable chapter in American art will result.

Patricia Trenton, Ph.D.   Patrick T. Houlihan, Ph.D.
Curator, LAACO Incorporated   Director, Southwest Museum
The Los Angeles Athletic Club Collection

Acknowledgments

Many individuals have generously supported this project, not only in Southern California but in the wider geography of the exhibition. A special expression of gratitude for their assistance in providing us with valuable information and materials is extended to the following: Suzanne Abel-Vidor, Interim Curator, The Sun House, Ukiah, California; Cheryl Bell, Assistant to Frank G. Hathaway, LAACO Incorporated; the Leandro Bernal family, Taos; Jack Boyer, Director, Kit Carson Memorial Foundation, Taos; Helen Greene Blumenschein, Taos; Searles R. Boynton, D.D.S., Ukiah; Sherry Brown, Tucson, Arizona; Edwin H. Carpenter, The Huntington Library, San Marino; Mary Cates, Curator, Blumenschein House, Kit Carson Memorial Foundation, Taos; Elizabeth Chatham, Santa Fe; Thomas M. Collins, Taos; Marilyn Concha, Taos; Zeb Connelly, Jamison Gallery, Santa Fe; Sue Critchfield, Librarian, Museum of New Mexico, Fine Arts Division, Santa Fe; Terry DeLapp, Los Angeles; Christine Doran, The Oakland Museum Art Department, Oakland, California; Peter Eickstaedt, Santa Fe; Forrest Fenn, Fenn Galleries, Ltd., Santa Fe; Martha Fleischman, Kennedy Galleries, New York; Lucy Fowler, School of American Research, Santa Fe; Eleanor Gehres, Head, and Staff, Denver Public Library, Western History Department, Denver; Stephen L. Good, Rosenstock Arts, Denver; Matilda Hadley, Taos; Ron Hall, Hall Galleries, Fort Worth; Warren Hanford, Santa Fe; Sarah J. Hatfield, San Jose, California; Paul Hernández, Los Angeles; Mark Hoffman, Maxwell Gallery, San Francisco; Paul Karlstrom, Director, and Staff, Archives of American Art, San Francisco; Virginia and Ernie Leavitt, Tucson; William Leisher, Los Angeles; Nettie Lujan, Taos; Edward Maeder, Los Angeles; Don Menveg, Los Angeles; Fred Meyer, Director, and Anne Morand, Curator, Thomas Gilcrease Institute of American History and Art, Tulsa, Oklahoma; Julie Montoya, Taos; Devin M. Oldendick, Assistant to the Reference Librarian, Cincinnati Art Museum Library, Cincinnati; Arthur L. Olivas, Photographic Archivist, Photo Archives, Museum of New Mexico, Santa Fe; William E. Paxson, Sr., and William E. Paxson, Jr., Los Angeles and Santa Barbara; Gerald P. Peters, Peters Corporation, Santa Fe; Steve Plattner, Photo Archivist, Cincinnati Historical Society; Will-Amelia Sterns Price, Santa Fe; Tina Ressa, Rialto, California; Tony Reyna, Past Governor of the Taos Pueblo and Former Regent of the University of New Mexico, Taos; Rick Romancito, Curator, Millicent Rogers Memorial Museum, Taos; Louis Romero, Taos; Roselea "Daisy" Mirabal Romero, Taos; Steve Rose, Biltmore Galleries, Los Angeles; Richard Rudisill, Curator, Photo Archives, Museum of New Mexico, Santa Fe; Polly Schaafsma, Laboratory of Anthropology, Museum of New Mexico, Santa Fe; Mary Concha Schlosser, Taos; Sherry Smith-Gonzáles, State Archivist, State Records Center and Archives, Santa Fe; Ray W. Steele, Director, C. M. Russell Museum, Great Falls, Montana; William W. Sturm, Librarian, Oakland History Room, Main Library, Oakland; Jackie Van Vliet, Pasadena; Robert White, Albuquerque; Arthur H. Wolf, Director, Millicent Rogers Memorial Museum, Taos; David Witt, Curator of Art, The Harwood Foundation, Taos.

Some individuals deserve particular recognition. We wish to acknowledge with special thanks the untiring efforts and able assistance of researchers Malin Wilson and Susan E. Nunemaker who gathered material on the Taos and

Santa Fe painters. Our editor, Jeanne D'Andrea, merits our respect for her expertise, judgment, and interest in the project; photographer Larry Reynolds is responsible for the excellent color transparencies; Owen Jones has met the challenge of a complex catalog design with an inventive solution; and Harry Montgomery, Typecraft Inc., has produced a beautiful catalog. Linda Taubenreuther reviewed and commented on the manuscript; and James Greaves used his fine expertise in conserving the works for the show. Karen Hathaway, Vice President and General Counsel, LAACO Incorporated, has generously consulted with us on legal matters for the catalog.

Our gratitude goes to the Southwest Museum for its able assistance during all phases of this project, above all to Peter Welsh, Gail Anderson, Sally Erickson, Dan Muenzberg, Jeannette Leeper, Claudine Scoville, Stephen LeBlanc, Maria Shufeldt, Daniela Moneta, and Yolanda Galvan. The continuing support of the Board of Trustees of the Southwest Museum and of its President, Dr. Norman F. Sprague, Jr., is gratefully acknowledged, as is our indebtedness to LAACO Incorporated for its generosity in underwriting the exhibition and its catalog. We especially congratulate Frank G. Hathaway, Chairman of the Board of Directors, LAACO Incorporated, whose high standards, foresight, and sensitivity to the arts made him a guiding spirit from the inception of this project.

California

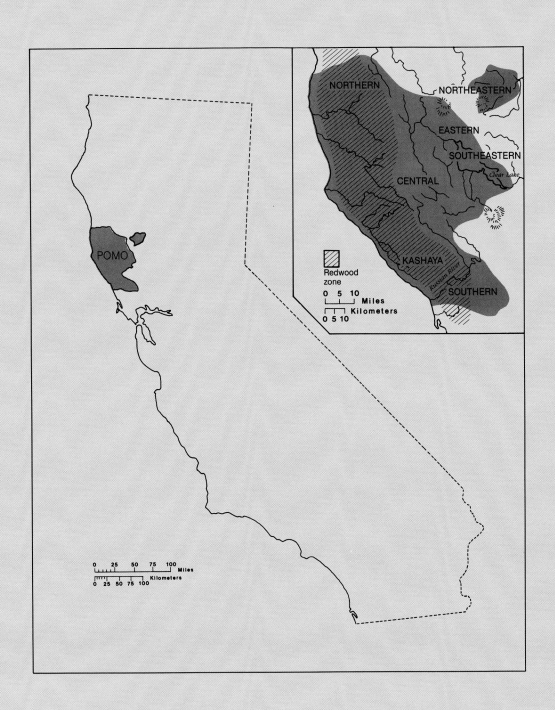

POMO

NORTHERN

NORTHEASTERN

EASTERN

SOUTHEASTERN

CENTRAL

Clear Lake

KASHAYA

Russian River

SOUTHERN

Redwood zone

0 5 10 Miles

0 5 10 Kilometers

0 25 50 75 100 Miles

0 25 50 75 100 Kilometers

The boundaries of the California culture area are not equivalent to the current state boundaries, which were established in 1852 when California entered the Union. Indeed, large eastern portions of the state are affiliated culturally with the Great Basin culture area as are major southern portions of the state with the Southwest culture area.

California is characterized by a great deal of environmental variation. Within its larger boundaries, regional culture areas are generally distinguished: Northwest California, Northeast California, the North Coast Range, the Sacramento Valley, the San Joaquin Valley, the South Coast Range, and the Southern Coast. The native cultures within these regions differed in part because of the resources available for exploitation. Thus the tribal groups in the Northwest developed extensive fishing practices in order to exploit the salmon runs in the river systems there. These practices differ considerably from the heavy dependence on acorns and hunted game of the tribes in the North Coast Range.

Tribal groups did not confine themselves to exploiting only one of these regions, and the uniformity of any given region should not be overstated. Indeed, there were important microenvironments within each region, and later discussions of the Pomo groups in the North Coast Range detail this variation.

Seven major language families or stocks are found among the sixty or so California tribes known to have existed in historic times. These include the Penutian, Hokan, Uto-Aztecan, Na Dene, Algic, and Yukian; and all have representative speakers in tribes found outside of California. It should be noted that more than 300 different dialects of these seven families or stocks were spoken in aboriginal California, attesting to the complex tapestry of this native American culture area.

Although Spanish explorers landed in Alta California as early as 1540, the first permanent European colony was not established in San Diego until 1769. The California Indian population at this later date has been estimated at 300,000, while that of 1900 is thought to be about 20,000, a decline of more than 90 percent in 130 years. The major causes of this decline are disease, military action, and destruction of native habitats resulting in starvation, exposure, and death.

Certainly the salient factor in cultural change for all native populations of California was the Spanish and later American colonization of the area. From 1769 to 1823 the Spaniards established a total of twenty-one missions along the coastal strip from San Diego to San Francisco. These missions took as their charge the relocation of the native populations as a means of converting and "civilizing" them. This forced relocation resulted in the deaths of tens of thousands of native Californians. Following Spanish and Mexican rule, American control of California, beginning in 1848, continued the destruction of native cultures. As had the Spaniards, the Americans enslaved, killed, and drove Indians off their traditional lands.

The Indians who survived this onslaught of European and American cultures were those who found refuge in isolated and/or undesirable locations throughout the culture area. Some of these areas in time became reservations, while others were parts of large tracts held by various governmental agencies.

Frank A. Schilling
In the Land of the Pomos
Southwest Museum Collection

Portrait of Henry Raschen
From the frontispiece of
Harry Flayderman, *Henry Raschen:
Painter of the American Indian*
(Privately Printed, 1958).
Courtesy the Oakland Museum Art
Department, Oakland, California

Raschen, *Pomo Interior, Fort Ross, California*   Trenton

German-born Henry Raschen emigrated with his parents to America in 1868. He returned to Europe twice to study at Munich's Royal Academy of Fine Arts, from 1875 to 1883 under Ludwig Loefftz and Wilhelm Lindenschmidt and then again from 1890 to 1894. During the later stay he accompanied fellow-student William Leigh (see catalog entry) on a sketching tour of Italy.[1] A comparison of works completed before and after this second period at the academy reveals considerable change in style and technique. His Indian scenes of northern California and Arizona painted between 1884 and 1890 exhibit the realistic style of painting Raschen had learned in his first study period—a tight and exactly detailed construction, based on the Old Masters, which was basic to the Munich training of that time. *Pomo Interior*, for example, exhibits these characteristics, in its extraordinary richness of realistic and ethnographic detail. His later works exhibit a broader manner of painting characterized by vigorous brushwork and dexterous handling of pigment, exemplified in his peasant subjects of Upper Bavaria.[2]

During the period 1884 to 1890, Raschen shared a studio in San Francisco with the landscapist Carl von Perbandt, and the two men made excursions to the Pomo country around Fort Ross, where Raschen had spent his childhood. There Raschen made a group of paintings of the Pomos, which he then worked up in his studio. They were exhibited in San Francisco at the Morris & Kennedy gallery in 1884 and 1886. *Pomo Interior* shows Raschen's familiarity with Pomo life and customs, including the interior of the winter redwood hut, the food, and the Pomo cooking methods. Much of the wealth of ethnographic detail revealed in this picture attests to the exceptional basketmaking skills of the Pomo. The artist has carefully detailed the costumes, too, indicating that we might be observing a Pomo Indian woman with a European child; the physiognomy suggests Russian descent, and the Russians were early settlers at Fort Ross. While the artist has left no record that identifies the models for this painting or others of Pomoan subjects, he nevertheless has given us an invaluable visual description of Pomo life, captured in an exact and technically proficient rendering.

Henry Raschen
Pomo Interior, Fort Ross, California, 1884
Oil on canvas
40¼ × 30 in. (102.3 × 76.2 cm.)
Los Angeles Athletic Club Collection

Hudson, *Ka-ma-ko-ya*   Trenton

California artist Grace Hudson, known for her Pomo Indian pictures, shared an interest in painting children with expatriate American artist Mary Cassatt. While Cassatt chose her subjects from upper middle-class Anglo families, Hudson selected her young models from among her Pomoan neighbors and friends on the rancherías in Ukiah and Potter Valley, California. Cassatt's interest lay in the subtle psychological interplay between her sitters; Hudson's portrayals, in contrast, are rather straightforward while including a sense of human warmth and feeling for her subjects. Besides capturing the mood and attitude of her Pomoan sitters, Hudson wanted to document her Indian neighbors and their culture, traditions, lore, and artifacts. Her ethnologist-collector husband, Dr. John Wilz Napier Hudson, whose extensive collection of Pomo baskets was sold to the Smithsonian Institution in 1916, undoubtedly encouraged her interest in Pomoan subjects. Like Cassatt, Hudson was devoted

Grace Hudson
Ka-ma-ko-ya
(*Found in the Brush*), 1904
Oil on canvas
23½ × 33 in. (59.7 × 83.8 cm.)
Los Angeles Athletic Club Collection

Portrait of Grace and John Hudson in the Artist's Studio, ca. 1895
Courtesy the Sun House, City of Ukiah, California

7

to children and might well have found in her paintings of them some compensation for her own childlessness.[1]

Raised in Ukiah, Hudson and her twin brother, Grant, grew up among their Pomoan neighbors. Their father, A. O. Carpenter, a photographer, editor, and publisher of a series of newspapers, and their mother came to this Northern California town in 1869, having first settled in Potter Valley where Grace and her brother were born in 1865. As a youngster, the artist showed an early propensity for drawing and was sent to the California School of Design in San Francisco after graduating from high school in 1879. From 1880 to 1884 she attended classes under the director, Virgil Williams, Domenico Tojetti, and Raymond Yelland, the noted regional marine painter. On graduation, she received the coveted Alvord Prize for best full-length crayon study. In 1889 she opened a studio in Ukiah and gave art lessons, the same year she met her future husband. After marriage to John Hudson, a practicing physician who eventually gave up medicine to pursue ethnology, she began devoting full time to painting the younger members of the Pomoan tribes of her native Mendocino County. Joseph Baird, a California historian, wrote that "she was particularly adept at capturing the elusive, half-sad and yet winsome moods of the very young."[2] The Hudsons' union of forty-five years developed into a long and sharing professional partnership based on a profound interest in the Pomoan Indians and their material culture.

Early in her career, when Hudson was asked by a critic how she was able to produce so many wonderful portraits of her young subjects, she responded,

> When I see a baby that I want to paint, I cannot borrow it for an indefinite period by telling its parents it's the sweetest thing on earth. I have to kidnap it first and then overcome the natural inclination of a baby to do everything except what is desired. There is a popular superstition among the Indians that . . . to be sketched or photographed is sure to bring some terrible calamity down on the head of the subject . . . When I want a subject, I first have to find a squaw with a papoose. If the child's face suits me, I enter into negotiations with the mother to do some work for me. . . . She leaves the baby strapped up in his basket and braced up against the side of the house. . . . The next maneuver is to get possession of that papoose.[3]

Hudson said she then promptly sketched the subject, coaxing it by various means into assuming the pose she desired. She undoubtedly gained the confidence of her Indian models, for most of her mature works seem well posed. According to her brother, Hudson like many artists of that time used photographs as an aid in completing her works.[4] It is interesting to speculate whether the artist may have used dolls on occasion as substitutes for her subjects (see Hudson studio photograph).

8

Several years after her marriage, Grace Hudson began to divide her time between painting in her Ukiah studio and accompanying her husband on anthropological outings. As her work load increased, she began to copyright her paintings and record them in a ledger by number, date, title, and subject, making it possible to identify her subjects by name, completion date, and title. During 1904, when *Ka-ma-ko-ya* was executed, the artist's ledger lists a record forty-two works. Most of her subjects were from the Mitchell, Duncan, and Peters families; all shared close ties with the Hudson-Carpenter family.

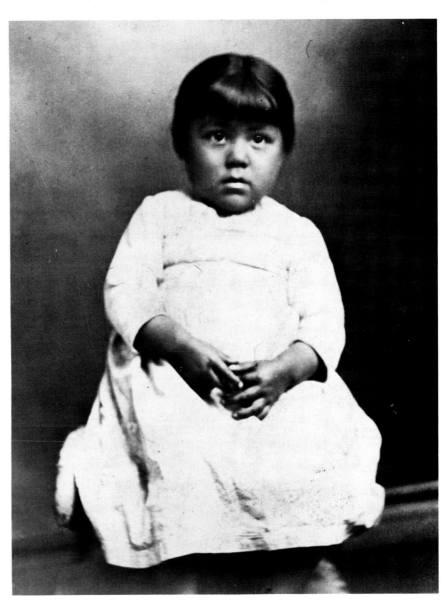

Portrait of Mary Angel Peters as a Child,
ca. 1897
Courtesy the Sun House, City of Ukiah,
California

It is impossible to know how Grace Hudson arrived at the title *Ka-ma-ko-ya*, since it does not spring from any known Pomo legend or myth about creation and birth, although according to her biographer, Searles R. Boynton, "The Pomo women . . . described their first children as 'being found in the brush.' "[5] We do know, however, that three of the five Peters children posed for this picture: Angel, the oldest, Rosita, the next in line, and William, the newborn baby.[6] All are prominently placed in the foreground, the eyes of the sisters directed tenderly toward the new member of their family, who more likely would have been bound in a cradle rather than in a fur. One might assume that his arrival was unexpected and the cradle basket not ready to receive him. Hudson has carefully interlocked her forms to create a harmonious figural grouping that is the central focus of this picture. Baskets and other background devices carry out the theme and add ethnological embellishment to the scene. The strong flood of light through the canvas opening of the shelter highlights the figures while casting reflections on the muddy ground and the large pot in the corner. Hudson was occasionally criticized for her sentimental portrayals. Here, we are less conscious of contrived charm and more drawn to the siblings' display of tenderness toward each other. Hudson has obviously captured her small subjects in relaxed and unself-conscious gestures: the satisfied expression in the face of the older sister, full of maternal pride; the younger sister curiously looking over her shoulder, attempting to fondle young William. While the painting is ethnologically interesting, the human qualities the artist has captured in this aesthetically composed picture are even more rewarding. Grace Hudson will be remembered in the annals of American art for her novel and interesting goal, the preservation of the Pomos in visual language.[7]

Storage Basket
Pomo
diam: 38 in; h: 20 in.
(96.6 cm.; 50.8 cm.)
Southwest Museum Collection

10

At the time of early contact with Europeans, perhaps as early as the sixteenth century, the California Indians we refer to as the Pomo occupied a territory north of San Francisco Bay within the modern boundaries of Mendocino, Sonoma, Lake, Glenn, and Coluss counties. This territory extended about 130 miles north to south and about 100 miles east to west, or just north of Point Reyes to Fort Bragg and from the Pacific Ocean to the Sacramento River. Although there were no census-takers in 1769 when the Spaniards first arrived in the San Francisco area, scholars today estimate the total Pomo population at that time to have been approximately 75,000 persons. This population remained relatively stable for about 100 years, until the enormous influx of Mexican and later American settlers caused a massive decline in Pomo population.

The aboriginal Pomo population was distributed across four topographic zones—the Coast, the Redwood Forest, the Valley Foothills, and the Lake Regions—that correspond to at least four different cultural patterns within an encompassing Pomo culture. Further complicating the picture of Pomo culture were the seven variations of the Pomo language, which itself was part of the Hokan family of languages. The distinctions among these seven languages were greater than dialect differences, and scholars today prefer to speak of the seven as comprising the Pomoan family of languages.

The paintings by Grace Hudson and Henry Raschen illustrate several aspects of Pomo culture. Raschen's scene in all likelihood presents a winter household of the Coast Pomo near Fort Ross, California. One can deduce this from the large quantity of sea foods heaped to the left of the seated figure as well as from the redwood slabs and bark of the house walls and roof. Only Pomo living along the coast or in the Redwood Forest had access to that particular wood as a building material; and of these two only the Coast Pomo had easy access to the sea foods shown here. Indeed, very few Pomo actually wintered in the redwood forests, preferring instead to exploit the resources of that area with seasonal forays. It is difficult to tell from the Raschen painting whether a central vertical pole supports the slanted sides and roof of the house or if the sides support each other, giving the house a wedgelike shape. Unlike the Coast Pomo, the Valley Pomo constructed conical winter houses of grasses, and the Lake Pomo used tule reeds as their principal building material.

All four Pomo groups utilized temporary shelters for seasonal subsistence activities, especially those resulting from freshwater fishing and acorn gathering. The Hudson painting probably depicts a temporary shelter used during early fall acorn gathering. Canvas or a similar fabric has been stretched to form a largely open-air windbreak. In Eastern Pomo dialect the term for the tenth moon of their lunar calendar translates "we will be camping and gathering acorns." The huge storage basket to the right of the figures in the Hudson picture held the acorns, while the mortar and basket to their left were essential parts of the equipment for processing the nuts. At least five different species of oak grow in the territory inhabited by Pomo, and the preparation of acorns for human consumption required leaching the tannic acid from the mortar-ground nutmeal.

All of the Pomo groups used acorns for food, but the Coast Pomo naturally relied most on the ocean's bounty. A careful examination of both the Hudson and the Raschen pictures provides an excellent overview of the marine and terrestrial ecologies exploited by the Pomo. Not shown are foods secured from a freshwater ecological base. Thus in addition to acorns and shellfish, we see rabbit and bird carcasses (possibly dove or pigeon), and raccoon, lynx, and other animal skins—probably sea otter or mink. The Raschen painting also refers to foods such as seaweed and kelp, seen overflowing the gathering basket to the left of the figures. The purple-red color of this ribbon-like substance is probably *Porphyra perforata*, a Pacific coastal seaweed that was preserved by sun drying and shaped into cakes for storage.

The bird feathers adorning the hanging basket in the Raschen painting provide the viewer with evidence of at least three bird species taken for their feathers. Their common names are redheaded woodpecker, yellowbreasted meadowlark, and blackheaded California quail. Other bird species were taken

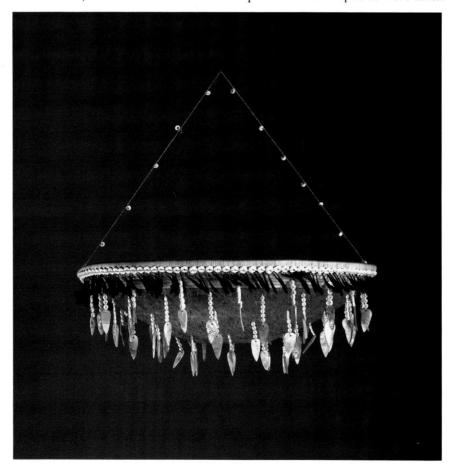

Feather Basket
Pomo
diam: 13 ½ in; h: 3 ¼ in.
(34.3 cm.; 8.3 cm.)
Southwest Museum Collection

Twined Basketry Start
Pomo
h: 22 in; finished portion: 5 in.
(55.9 cm.; 12.7 cm.)
Southwest Museum Collection

for black feathers, especially the valley and mountain quail. This feathered container is generally considered a presentation basket, woven or commissioned, for example, to be presented at the birth of a child. Frequently, such a basket would be destroyed upon the owner's death.

The Raschen and the Hudson paintings illustrate well the most important art of the California Indians—basketry. Indian basketmakers of California far exceeded all other Indian basketmakers of native North America in artistry, methods of manufacture, and use of materials. And within California the most prolific basketmakers were the Pomo Indians. Artistically, their baskets are considered among the finest made in the state.

The Pomo employed basketry to produce an enormous range of implements and utensils for the gathering, transport, storage, preparation, cooking, and serving of food. In addition, baskets cradled infants, held ceremonial paraphernalia, and wrapped the dead. One scholar concluded that "from birth to death a Pomo used basketry for every possible purpose." As important, perhaps, as the proliferation of basketry, is its place in Pomo cosmology. Basketry was a gift of *Marumda*, the mythic hero in Pomo creation, during the fifth and final creation of the world. Marumda is responsible for the earlier four creations and destructions of the universe, and historic Pomos saw themselves as living in Marumda's fifth creation. Marumda is said to have given *kuhum* (the generic Pomo term for basketry material) to women at this time. He also directed them to willow as a basketry resource material, separating it from other raw materials associated with basketmaking.

13

Three Pomo techniques of basketry manufacture are known: twining, coiling, and wickerwork, and the first two are more common. Five distinct forms of twining were practiced: plain, diagonal, lattice, three-strand, and three-strand braided. Two coiling methods were known, one on a single rod and the other on a three-rod foundation. Twining may be described as a weaving process and coiling as a sewing process. In the Hudson painting one can see the start of a twined basket. The forest of twigs that extends vertically above the finished portion of the basket is the warp, or stationary element in the weaving process. The weft material that encircles these warp elements is necessarily pliable and usually worked wet to increase its flexibility. The direction of movement of this weft element usually indicates whether the weaver was a man or a woman.

Another interesting feature of Pomo basketry is the fact that only men produce certain types of baskets, namely fish traps, baby carriers, and coarse openwork forms for storage or transport. Not only did Pomo men and women make different types of baskets but there was also a sexual division of labor based on method of manufacture. All close-woven (or coiled) baskets were the product of female weavers, and most open-weave baskets of twining or wickerwork were made by male weavers. Curiously missing from the inventory of baskets in these two paintings is the twined Pomo baby carrier, despite the presence of a nursing infant in the Hudson painting. The infant is, however, tightly wrapped in a skin that acted as a cushion in such a basketry baby carrier.

The surface designs of Pomo basketry result from different manufacturing techniques. In twined basketry, horizontal designs are more common than parallel or diagonal or crossing diagonal ones. In coiled basketry, horizontal designs occur more frequently than parallel diagonal, crossing diagonal, vertical, or separate groups of design patterns.

Of the baskets seen in these two paintings only the feathered one in the Raschen can definitely be said to be coiled work. The Pomo sewed feathers only to coiled baskets and, further, only to three-rod coiled baskets. All of the others are probably twined.

Two of the baskets are depicted with fairly clear designs. In the Hudson painting the large acorn storage basket has three separate bands of horizontal decoration, and in the Raschen the feathered basket has diagonal patterning. Although in both paintings the basketry designs are difficult to distinguish, the design bands of the large basket in the Hudson painting probably would not completely encircle the basket. The design would be broken at a point that the Pomo would call a *dau*, *ham*, or *hwa*; failure to leave such a break would result in blindness to the weaver. At the turn of the century, researchers at the University of California, Berkeley, sought to identify the Pomo terms for all of the known basketry designs by Pomo weavers. Of a total of approximately forty-six named designs, only twenty-six were in common usage. Twenty of these twenty-six were in the language spoken in the northern dialect, seventeen in the central, and fourteen in the eastern.

The clearest indication of a basketry design in the two paintings is that on the hanging feather basket in the Raschen: a series of yellow rectangles moves

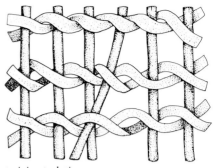

twining technique

coiling technique

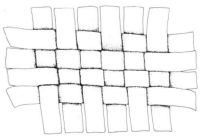

plaiting technique

Basketry Techniques. Fig. 2. Detail: twining technique. Fig. 3. Detail: coiling technique; a. grass foundation, b. three-rod foundation. Fig. 4. Detail: plaiting technique. Courtesy Christopher Moser, *Rods, Bundles, and Stitches* (Riverside, Ca.: Riverside Museum Press, 1981). Illustrations by Debra Turnbull.

14

diagonally across a red field that encircles the basket. This is a relatively common design in Pomo basketry and carries two names. For Pomoan speakers of the Northern and Central areas it is *bice-mao* and *pce-mao*, respectively, and both translate as "deer-back." For Eastern Pomo speakers it is *du-dile* or "potato-forehead." In all three dialects, however, when the rectangles are very small the design is called *bitu'mtu* or "ants." Frequently a string of connected rectangles will occur with other elements that make up a much more complex design. The designs on the large storage basket in the Hudson painting are visible but not in enough detail for accurate analysis. I would call attention to the interesting use of positive and negative designs in the triangles that make up the central design band.

Also of interest is the metal cooking pot in the Raschen painting, which is clearly a trade item to the Pomo. Prior to contact with Europeans, basketry containers served as cooking vessels and the heat source was from fire-heated stones that were placed on wooden racks within the basketry container. Of European character, too, is the woman's costume in the Raschen. The picture is thought to have been painted near Fort Ross, the site of the former Russian Colony in California, and this may account for the style of the dress. Both

Twined Basket
Pomo
h: 14 in.
(35.6 cm.)
Southwest Museum Collection

Glass Beads
Russian or Spanish trade goods
l. overall: 24¾ in.
(62.9 cm.)
Southwest Museum Collection

paintings show some of the personal adornment worn by adult women and children. The child in the Raschen picture wears an abalone shell necklace and the woman a headdress of woodpecker feathers. The feathered band of the headdress extends about three-quarters of the way around the head and is tied by a string at the back. In the Hudson painting, the young woman holding the child wears a string of red beads that are probably of European glass manufacture and not of native shell. Nor are the costumes in these paintings native dress; rather they reflect cultural change among the Pomo.

Southwest

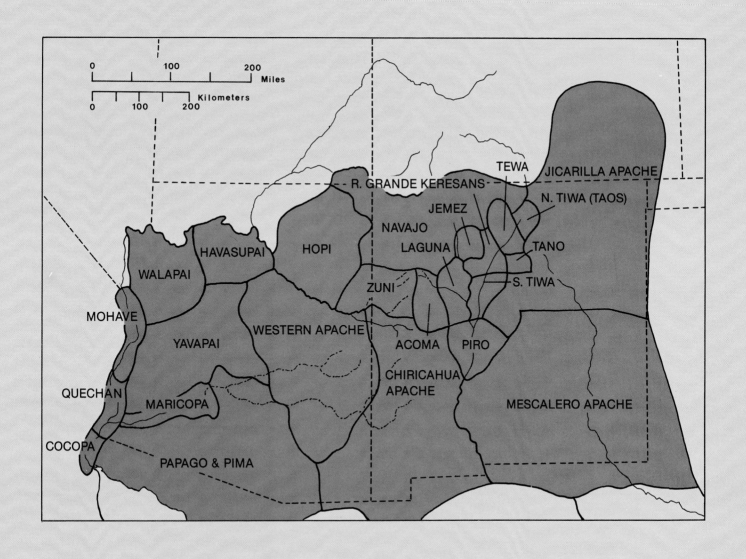

0 100 200 Miles

0 100 200 Kilometers

WALAPAI

HAVASUPAI

HOPI

R. GRANDE KERESANS

JEMEZ

NAVAJO

LAGUNA

ZUNI

TEWA

JICARILLA APACHE

N. TIWA (TAOS)

TANO

S. TIWA

MOHAVE

YAVAPAI

WESTERN APACHE

ACOMA

PIRO

CHIRICAHUA
APACHE

MESCALERO APACHE

QUECHAN

MARICOPA

COCOPA

PAPAGO & PIMA

The area designated as the Southwest can be confusing, and often a compound term is employed for clarification: the American Southwest or the Greater Southwest. At issue are the boundaries of this culture area, and to provide easily recognizable cornerstones, American and Mexican state borders are often cited. Thus the southern portions of Nevada, Utah, and Colorado, and all of Arizona and New Mexico, are said to comprise the American Southwest. These states, and the Mexican states of Sonora, Chihuahua, Sinaloa, and Durango, are the usual contemporary political units that encompass the Greater Southwest.

Within these boundaries are three outstanding physical features: mountains (the southern Rockies and the Sierra Madre Occidental), deserts (the Sonoran and Chihuahuan), and the Colorado Plateau. They are extremely useful in describing the development of the area's prehistoric Indian cultures, for the major prehistoric cultures, Mogollon, Hohokam, and Anasazi, evolved initially in the mountain, desert, and plateau environments respectively. Across all three of these land forms the major climatic feature is aridity.

The dominant cultural features of the historic Indian cultures of the Southwest include agriculture—the triad of corn, beans, and squash, settled villages unique to the Pueblos, an elaborate ceremonial life, and numerous artistic achievements. Among the best known of the resident Indian tribes are the Pueblo people, and they typify the popular image of Southwestern Indians. Today we refer to these Indians as "pueblo," the Spanish term for town, because of the distinctions made by the early Spanish officials between settled, agricultural Indians and other less stable tribes of hunters and gatherers, such as the Navajo and Apache, and still other agriculturalists, such as the Pima and Papago of southern Arizona. These latter agricultural tribes were referred to by the Spaniards as *ranchería* people, because their preferred settlement pattern was one of discrete farming sites along river or irrigation water courses; and they often migrated seasonally to higher elevations on the Sonoran Desert, whereas the Pueblos remained in their village sites year round.

In the Los Angeles Athletic Club Collection only the Pueblo Indians of the Southwest are represented in paintings, and of the two dozen or so Pueblo groups still extant, Taos and Hopi Pueblos are the only tribal subjects represented in the selections here. In fact, there may have been a subject preference among late nineteenth- and early twentieth-century American artists for these two pueblos that helps to explain their sole presence in this collection as well as their predominance in most other collections of Southwest painting.

The interest in Taos Pueblo and the presence nearby of an "artist colony" is explained in part by the close proximity of the Santa Fe Railroad. The pervasive Spanish culture in juxtaposition to the Pueblo Indian culture in that region of New Mexico also attracted many well-traveled artists, as did the quality of the natural light and the physical setting. The serene monumentality of the mountain backdrop for the four- and five-story Taos Pueblo undoubtedly pleased the discerning eye of many artists, too. Whatever the reasons, Taos

Pueblo is widely celebrated in American art and the selections here from the Los Angeles Athletic Club Collection reflect this attraction.

Some of these same conditions also attracted many artists to Hopi. After about 1890 the Santa Fe Railroad could be traveled easily across northern Arizona, as could the later automobile roadways linking the Hopi Mesas with the Grand Canyon to the north and the transcontinental highway (Route 66) to the south. Although there are no dramatic backdrop mountains, the Hopi Mesas are also compellingly beautiful to most artists. In addition, the Hopi probably seemed quite exotic to many artists, who were further entranced by Hopi ritual practices, particularly those of the Kachina Cult and the Snake Dance.

Both Hopi and Taos Pueblos have been very heavily photographed, too, at least in the late nineteenth and early twentieth century. There are numerous photographs depicting large concentrations of photographers at Indian activities, especially Kachina and Snake Dance rituals at Hopi. Such historic photographs were frequently used by painters in search of subject matter for their art. Disruptive photographers prompted both pueblos to restrict photography early in this century, at Hopi, for example, by 1911.

Hopi Snake Dance, Oraibi, ca. 1900
George Wharton James Collection
Southwest Museum

Hopi Pueblo   Houlihan

The Hopi Indians live in north-central Arizona on or about three mesas that overlook the Colorado Plateau. They have lived there for more than 1,000 years, and their prehistoric ancestors are called Anasazi. The Hopi living atop the mesas are a few hundred feet higher than the surrounding plateau, and the mesas are named in order of their occurrence from east to west as First Mesa, Second Mesa, and Third Mesa. In fact, these mesas are best thought of as fingers of high ground that jut out to the south from a large landform—the Black Mesa, all of which is a part of the Colorado Plateau.

On or near these three mesas are twelve Hopi communities whose 6,000 inhabitants speak a Uto-Aztecan language. Linguists concerned with the Hopi language have identified four dialects that are mutually intelligible: First Mesa, Mishongnovi, Shipaulovi, and Third Mesa.

As do the other Pueblo tribes to the east, the Hopi practice agriculture, growing a variety of vegetable crops (corn, beans, squash, melons, and chiles), cotton, and fruit trees (especially peaches and apricots). In order to grow these crops they have developed agricultural techniques that cope with their arid environment. In addition to floodwater farming and irrigation agriculture, the Hopi plant such deep-rooting crops as beans, corn, and fruit trees in the sand dunes at the bases of the mesas. These sand-dune fields are protected with

Charles F. Lummis
Hopi Village of Walpi, 1891
Southwest Museum Collection
(neg. no. 24085)

windbreaks constructed of rocks and brush to prevent the desert winds from constantly reshifting the land. Although the Hopi have had livestock since the arrival of the Spaniards, these animals are of considerably less cultural importance for the Hopi than for their neighbors, the Navajos.

Unlike the Eastern Pueblos along the Rio Grande and its tributaries, the Hopi depend on a much less predictable water supply for their crops. In response to the uncertainty of water, they have developed an elaborate set of ritual complexes to induce rain and to provide fertility and good harvests. Primary among these rituals is the Kachina Cult. While Kachinas are present in all of the Pueblos, the Kachina Cult is much more elaborate for such Western Pueblos as Hopi, Zuni, and Acoma. In one sense, the term Kachina refers to a generalized spiritual being that controls rain. In another sense, the term may refer to the masked dancers that impersonate these spiritual beings in rituals during the months between the winter solstice in December and the middle of July, a few weeks after the summer solstice. The goal of these and other ritual practices is to bring rain to their fields and thus sustain the Hopi people.

Hopi social organization is extremely complex and is interwoven with political as well as religious offices and functions. Thus each village contains households, kivas, clan groups, and ceremonial societies that crisscross the social, political and religious affiliations of each resident Hopi. In addition to these traditional structures, there has been a tribal council with representatives from each village since the Indian Reorganization Act became law in 1934.

The traditional arts of the Hopi include painted pottery, textiles, basketry, jewelry, and wood sculpture, for example, kachina dolls. Since the late 1890s the demand for these works has grown steadily, and many Hopi support themselves and their families by extensive craft sales. Compounding an already complex political and social structure are several craft marketing groups, such as the Hopi Silvercraft Cooperative.

William Leigh traveled from the jungles of Africa to the deserts of the Southwest to gather material for his highly charged, romantic, and imaginative storytelling paintings of primitive man living harmoniously with nature. His biographers have already noted that, given his childhood in the postwar South and his inherent sensibilities, he could hardly have "viewed the world other than romantically however real the turmoil that overwhelmed the South at the time of his birth" in 1866.[1] In later reminiscences about his childhood rambles on his family's impoverished plantation in his native West Virginia, Leigh describes a locally famous spring; its waters, issuing from a rock cliff, "excited the imagination. This lulling music produced a strange sense of beauty and mystery. . . . The voice of Nature, telling of caverns and weird channels which no human eye had ever beheld; what fabulous fairy tales—could we but comprehend its words—might it convey to our dull, prosaic minds."[2] This early propensity for the romantic was reinforced later by Leigh's academic training at the Royal Academy of Fine Arts in Munich, where his fondness for genre and narrative were cultivated.

Leigh first visited the Southwest in 1906. This trip and subsequent ones established his passion for the region and its native inhabitants, and his course veered from that of illustrator to painter of Southwestern genre. In the company of Albert Groll, a fellow student in Munich, Leigh visited the Indian pueblos at Laguna, Zuni, and Acoma. It was Acoma that he chose as a backdrop for his *Pool at Oraibi*, a Hopi subject. He recorded it as "wildly picturesque and weirdly dramatic [this] 'Enchanted Mesa,' " a place "like a fantastic dream," in a series of oil studies and photographs that served as memory jottings for the pictures he later assembled in his New York studio. Here, the sandstone cliffs and the ledge surrounding the small pool of water are similar to photographic studies he made at Acoma.[3]

The artist first saw the Navajo country and the Hopi mesas in 1912, when he headquartered at the well-known trading post of Don Lorenzo Hubbell in Ganado, Arizona, a hospitable mecca for writers and artists. He and two companions secured an adobe house at the foot of the First Mesa, and, he said, "painted studies incessantly . . . I was eager to waste no time whatever; I saw that I needed studies of everything—the vegetation, the rocks, the plains, the mesas, the sky, the Indians, and their dwellings. . . . I saw that I must so far as possible be a sponge, soak up everything I saw; must know the manners and customs of the people and their employment." Detailed sketches of Indian life and settlements as well as plant and animal life of the desert filled his portfolios. They provided inspiration for some of the Southwestern works he exhibited at Snedecor-Babcock Gallery in New York in January and February 1918. *Pool at Oraibi* was among these paintings.[4]

Leigh's ideas and ideals were highly controversial and were expressed in his many published writings, but they can be tied to his art in only a limited way. "Individualism was the most pronounced trait in Leigh's character and a theme repeatedly appearing throughout his writings. 'Great things are done by

William Leigh
Pool at Oraibi, 1917
Oil on canvas
22½ × 28¼ in. (57.2 × 71.3 cm.)
Los Angeles Athletic Club Collection

single persons,' he wrote, 'never by mobs.' "[5] He believed that one way to protect individuality was to be vigilant about one's self-respect. His beliefs on individualism manifest themselves in many of his paintings: a single figure carries the qualities of human dignity, self-respect, and total harmony with nature. Leigh's beautiful Hopi maiden idyllically pictured by a pool radiates these qualities. Her primitive way of life, her tranquillity, and her oneness with nature express Leigh's conviction that the worth of an individual exceeds that of society. It hardly matters whether the artist drew on his fertile imagination or on historic photographs for his picturemaking. His deeply held philosophies were so subtly interwoven in his storytelling pictures that these works cannot be summarily labeled as illustrations.

Leigh's respect for the idealized human body is evident in this and many of his other Indian paintings. His technical proficiency in drawing the human figure enabled him to visually express his ideals. Although lauded for their

Leigh in His New York Studio
Courtesy the Thomas Gilcrease Institute of American History and Art, Tulsa, Oklahoma

24

draftsmanship, his pictures were often criticized unjustly for their want or quality of color. Yet the same critics praised the smooth, mellow flesh tones of his Indian subjects, comparing them to the pretty peasant maids of the French artist Bouguereau. One has only to observe the skillful application of vibrant color and use of light in *Pool at Oraibi* to appreciate the artist's mastery of paint and brushwork. The beautifully orchestrated colors and the strong play of light and dark create a harmonious whole, transporting us back to another era that was characterized by a sense of spirituality and mystery. For Leigh, however, "the human message in a picture—the story telling qualities of human joys and sorrows, the tragedies and poetry of life, the problems of the world"—were more important than technical execution.[6] Leigh has created a romantic scene that is both primitive and sublime: the young Hopi maiden caught up in deepest revery, skillfully conveys the artist's message of human dignity.

Frederick Monsen
Hopi Woman Filling a Water Jar
Southwest Museum Collection
(neg. no. 24080)

Leigh, *Pool at Oraibi*   Houlihan

Pool at Oraibi is a wonderful combination of fact and fiction. With the exception of the water site it has excellent ethnographic accuracy in the young Hopi woman's costume, her hair style, and the water container she is about to fill.

The fiction: there are three sources of water at Oraibi, the Third Mesa community that is said to be the setting for this painting of 1917. There is a tank in the center of Oraibi, there are a few cisterns to the north of the town, and there are two or three wells, or seeps, at the base of the Mesa. The pool of water in the painting resembles none of them and in all likelihood was the creation of the artist, quite possibly patterned after similar pool sites at Zuni and Acoma Pueblos. Several well-known turn-of-the-century photographs by Adam Clark Vroman, George Wharton James, Edward S. Curtis, and Frederick Monsen depict Pueblo women taking water from these pools, and it is possible that Leigh used these Acoma or Zuni sites for his Hopi maiden.

Despite the fanciful nature of the water source, Leigh's depiction of the Hopi woman's dress is excellent. Prior to the presence of the Spaniards in the Southwest, such dresses were woven of cotten and dyed dark brown or black. After the Europeans came, sheep's wool replaced cotton as the raw material for these dresses. The woman's dress is actually a single large piece of cloth that was woven by men. The only added decoration is the green and red piping, and the red shoulder stitching shown here holds the dress over the right shoulder. The left side of the dress is fitted against the body, under the arm.

Edward S. Curtis
Acoma Woman at a Well
Southwest Museum Collection
(neg. no. 24079)

Embroidered Border (detail)
Woman's dress
Hopi
Southwest Museum Collection

Canteen
Hopi
h: 12½ in.
(31.8 cm.)
Southwest Museum Collection

Adam Clark Vroman
Creating a Hopi Maiden's Hair Whorl, 1901
Southwest Museum Collection
(neg. no. 22577)

Sash
Pueblo or Navajo
7 ft. 8 in. × 5 in.
(243.9 × 12.7 cm.)
Southwest Museum Collection

A curious aspect of the Hopi woman's dress is that prior to its use as a dress, the same piece of weaving would be used as a cape. In its use as a cape it lacks the piping and the only design detail is a weaving pattern change on the sides, which is not shown here. The sash that wraps about the waist is typical of the sashes or belts that also were woven by men, of either cotton or wool.

The water containers shown here may not both be ceramic. The dipper may have been of wood, a gourd, or of fired clay. Without question the canteen is ceramic, and virtually the same form is used on all three mesas. Clay for these canteens is gathered by potters from clay beds at the foot of each mesa. Ground potsherds are added to the clay as a temper. Canteens like this will hold several quarts, and they become quite heavy when full. They are carried on the back by means of a woven strap that fits across the forehead and attaches to the handles opposite the opening of the canteen.

The woman's hair style is that of an unmarried woman who is old enough to marry. It is arranged in a distinctive whorl pattern that is formed with the help of another woman by wrapping the long hair over a bent U-shaped stick. The pattern is popularly referred to as the "butterfly whorl."

Taos Pueblo   Houlihan

About seventy miles north of Santa Fe, New Mexico, Taos is the northernmost of the Tiwa Pueblos. As such it is one of three groups of pueblos related by language. Its linguistic affiliates include the nearby Picuris Pueblo to the south, the more distant Sandia and Isleta Pueblos north and south of Albuquerque, respectively, and Indian communities in Texas, near El Paso, and in northern Chihuahua, Mexico. Taos is also the name of the Anglo and Hispanic city 2.8 miles south of Taos Pueblo.

The geographic position of Taos Pueblo is essential to any understanding of its history and culture. Taos Pueblo is situated on a broad well-watered plateau at the base of the Sangre de Cristo mountain range to the northeast. In the past these mountains afforded easy access to deer, elk, bear, turkey, grouse, and squirrel. Beyond them to the northeast the Taos hunted buffalo on the Plains; on the sagebrush land to the west they caught rabbit and antelope. In addition to hunting, trout were taken in the numerous streams and rivers that drained the mountains, and many species of wild plants were gathered. By comparison with the more southern pueblos, Taos relied much less on agriculture, because of its shorter growing season, a more erratic weather pattern, and the abundance of game and wild foods.

Prior to the coming of Spanish settlers, Taos agriculture like that of the Hopi consisted of corn, beans, and squash. As a result of Spanish contact other crops, especially wheat, were cultivated. Perhaps more important were the additions to Taos Pueblo life of domesticated animals such as horses, cattle, pigs, and donkeys. Today wage labor is of even greater importance than hunting, farming, and ranching.

The spiritual sustenance of the Pueblo is to be found in the mountains. There the winter snows are gathered in numerous lakes, especially Blue Lake, which drains through the Pueblo as the Rio Pueblo de Taos. Blue Lake supplies both the drinking and irrigation water for the Pueblo, and the lake itself is considered of immense spiritual consequence to the Taos. Each summer in August, adult men and women from the Pueblo travel to Blue Lake for rituals that are considered necessary to the Pueblo's welfare. Since the arrival of the Spaniards in the sixteenth century, the people of Taos have maintained their Pueblo religious traditions and mingled them with Christianity.

Beyond the mountains to the northeast are the Great Plains, and relations between the tribes on the Plains and the Taos have not always been peaceful. Still the contact between the two groups has resulted in substantial exchanges of cultural traits that still persist in Taos today. A number of these traits will be discussed in conjunction with some of the paintings, although the most visible cultural borrowings evident in these paintings are in costume, hairstyle, and certain aspects of ritual.

Since the Civil War the estimated population of Taos has climbed steadily. Figures show Taos's population to have increased almost four hundred percent in this century. The pueblo of Taos is actually three settlements: North House, South House (both within the historic walls), and the scattered and separated houses outside these walls. Dividing North House and South House is the Rio Pueblo de Taos, an eastern tributary of the Rio Grande. The low wall encircling the pueblo proper is the remains of a defensive redoubt known to have been used in the 1700s to repel attacks by Plains Indians. Consistent with the need for defense, before about 1800 Taos built no ground-floor entrances, and access to lower-level dwellings was limited to roof openings. These roof accesses were reached by ladders, which were pulled up onto the roofs in the event of an attack by warring neighbors. The people of Taos believe that the properties within the pueblo wall are sacred. Beyond the walls new, separated housing occupies former agricultural and grazing lands that were once held in common.

As evidence of the change in residence patterns at Taos Pueblo, we should consider that the number of households in 1936 at North House and South House within the walled Pueblo was 175, and only summer or ranch residences were located outside of the walls. In 1971 the number of households within the walls was 109, while 192 permanent houses were located outside of the walls. Clearly, along with population growth there has been a change in the preferred location of housing. Many of the new houses beyond

Charles F. Lummis
Taos Pueblo from the Northeast,
ca. 1887-96
Southwest Museum Collection
(neg. no. 24083)

the walls have fenced yards, flower beds, non-adobe construction, indoor baths and utilities, and household appliances, all foreign to the traditional households in North and South House. Thus the Taos Pueblo of today is very different in physical appearance from the one known by the artists of the Taos Society who used it as setting for a number of paintings in this exhibition. See Elsie Clews Parsons, *Taos Pueblo*, General Series in Anthropology, no. 2 (Menasha, Wisc.: 1936).

Charles F. Lummis
South House, Taos Pueblo,
ca. 1887-96
Southwest Museum Collection
(neg. no. 24084)

Sharp, *Shelling Corn*   Trenton

Although Sharp did not settle permanently in Taos until about 1909, his enthusiasm for the small Spanish-American village, near the great pueblo with its colorful inhabitants, launched the beginnings of the Taos Art Colony. After visiting there with his friend Cincinnati-artist John Hauser in summer 1893,[1] he spoke glowingly of its attractions to Ernest Blumenschein and Bert Phillips, his classmates at the Académie Julian in Paris, and convinced them to make a sketching tour through the Southwest. During that trip, in 1898, they were introduced to Taos by a fortunate accident, when their wagon broke down near Questa.[2] From this early discovery the art colony grew and attracted other Eastern artists who quickly became aware of the area's picturesque possibilities. In July 1915, Sharp, Blumenschein, Phillips, Berninghaus, Couse, and W. Herbert Dunton founded the Taos Society of Artists in order to organize traveling exhibitions and spread the word about Taos.[3]

Like other early artist-illustrators who settled in Taos, Sharp wanted to preserve some of the traditional Indian customs before they were lost in a period of rapid change. Although he was an accurate recorder and student of the Indian, Sharp, like his fellow artists, had a tendency to idealize and romanticize his subjects, focusing on the exotic and picturesque aspects of their culture. In his elaborate studio pictures, seated or standing Indians—illuminated, somewhat depersonalized, and surrounded by the necessary storytelling

Joseph Sharp
Shelling Corn, ca. 1925
Oil on canvas
40 × 48 in. (101.1 × 121.9 cm.)
Los Angeles Athletic Club Collection

Sharp in His Taos Studio Surrounded by His Artifact Collection
Courtesy Fenn Galleries, Ltd., Archives, Sharp Collection, Santa Fe

33

Bert Phillips, *Corn Husking Series*, ca. 1925
Courtesy Blumenschein House, Kit Carson
Memorial Foundation, Taos

34

props—perform a ceremonial rite or an activity of daily life. In a facile, academic style characteristic of the international mode of academic realism of the late nineteenth century, and undoubtedly inspired by his study abroad, Sharp painted scenes of Indian life rich in authentic ethnographic detail and nostalgic in mood. In *Shelling Corn* (ca. 1925), as in his other major compositions, the artist places his figures on a proscenium or stagelike structure. Symmetrically disposed around a large, black storage pot, the figures are compressed in a corner around a fireplace and illuminated from above by light from a special window designed by Sharp. The slightly upward-tilting plane of the bold, handsome Navajo rug lowers the viewer's vantage point, a modern device probably adapted by Sharp to show off his sitters and the Indian paraphernalia surrounding them. The compressed background gives the figures prominence in the foreground plane, a scheme Sharp repeatedly used in his studio compositions. The setting for this picture and many of his others is the artist's two-story adobe studio, built next to his home in 1915.[4]

When we compare the activity in the painting to the actual process of husking corn, seen in a series of photographs taken by Bert Phillips in the 1920s, it is evident that Sharp's version is staged and idealized.[5] Yet though Sharp has taken certain artistic liberties, *Shelling Corn* is one of his most accomplished painterly works, deeply expressing his nostalgia for the romantic past.

Sharp, *Shelling Corn*   Houlihan

Both of the Southwestern paintings by Sharp in this exhibition are set in the artist's own studio, although in *Shelling Corn* the fireplace is shown. Some of Sharp's extensive artifact collection is worn by his models, while other parts of it are incorporated as accessories appropriate to the scene. In both pictures the Pueblo woman's dress, belt, and boots are probably the same, and Sharp has seated the man and woman of *Shelling Corn* on the same low masonry bench.

Within this painting two pieces of blackware appear—one above the fireplace and the other in the center of the painting. The piece on the mantle ledge appears to be a "stew bowl"—a shape often thought to have been introduced by the Spaniards. The large jar is often referred to as an *olla*, or storage jar, and

Storage Jar
Santa Clara Pueblo
h: 20 in.
(50.8 cm.)
Southwest Museum Collection

Rug
Navajo
108 × 60 in.
(274.4 × 152.5 cm.)
Southwest Museum Collection

its function is suggested by the woman shelling corn. This large pot was probably made in Santa Clara Pueblo, to the south of Taos Pueblo. The presence of so-called bear paw impressions on the shoulder of the pot identifies it as a Santa Clara vessel. Among the explanations for this design is the oral tradition that the Santa Clara people were lost and that a bear led them back to their pueblo. While the historical facts of this tradition are not known, the bear is honored by incising its paw print in the pottery. This Santa Clara storage pot is placed on a Navajo rug of a style made at about the turn of the century.

In contrast to this Navajo textile are two Pueblo weavings—the woman's dress and her belt. Unlike the rug, which was woven by a Navajo woman, Pueblo textiles are woven by men. Another contrast is in the wool yarn used by the Navajo as opposed to the cotton used by the Pueblo weaver.

I believe that the pipe, the pipe bag, and the leggings are of Southern Plains and not Pueblo manufacture. Nonetheless, they could have been acquired by trade between a Taos and a Southern Plains Indian. Here, of course, we suspect that they belong to the artist and not the model. The leggings, however, might well belong to the man and not to Sharp. The casual handling of the pipe, and presumably of smoking itself, is quite fanciful on Sharp's part. Smoking such a pipe was an act of religious consequence, and neither this act nor the casual placement of the pipe bag on the floor is a true indication of the serious religious value given to this artifact by either the Pueblo or the Plains Indians.

Although the detail is not good, it seems likely that the two baskets shown are of coiled manufacture, probably by Jicarilla or Mescalero Apache basketmakers. Again, although both groups are located in New Mexico, and they traded extensively with Pueblo Indians, the baskets probably belonged to Sharp and not to the woman.

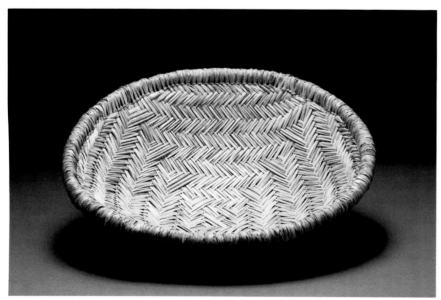

Plaited Basket
Hopi
diam: 20 in; h: 5¾ in.
(50.8 cm.; 14.7 cm.)
Southwest Museum Collection

Embroidered Border (detail)
Woman's dress
Pueblo
Southwest Museum Collection

After Sharp established permanent residence in Taos, he devoted much of his time to painting the Pueblo Indians, primarily depicting scenes from their ceremonial and daily lives. Although he continued to paint canvases of Plains Indian life from his sketches and memories, he often employed Taos models in these pictures, combining their distinctive hairdress with Plains-like clothing and artifacts. Sharp realized that the twentieth-century Indian was living in an age of transition—"the real, picturesque Indian was fast disappearing"—and thus was aware of the immediacy of his mission. He remarked with regret, "The small boys wear short hair and a shirt, while the girls are tidied up and in calico. It is heartbreaking to the artist, and particularly so if he has not had foresight to collect costumes and various artifacts which become more rare each year."[1]

Because of his benign and gentle nature and his deep compassion for the Indian, Sharp made close and lasting friendships with his Taoseño models. Among the many who often posed for him were John Gómez (Bird), Jerry Mirabal (Elkfoot), Frank Martínez (Bawling Deer), Francisco (Deer Coming), and his favorite female model, Crucita (New Corn). Sharp's sales ledger reveals that Crucita posed for many of his pictures from about 1915 until the time of her marriage in 1924.[2] Several of these paintings exist today, affording us the opportunity to see the different ways Sharp posed his model: alone, either with or without pictorial devices or accessories, and together with another of his favorite models. Interestingly, Crucita is usually costumed in the same Pueblo dress shown here, either with or without her colored undergarment. She wears the typical Taos boots, and her hair is dressed in bangs and caught up in a bun at the nape of her neck. Despite the artist's comments about the difficulty Indians had in unbending while posing,[3] Crucita appears relaxed and contemplative in most of these paintings. She was undoubtedly a natural model, totally at ease and oblivious to her role. Clearly, for this reason Sharp painted her often.

Here, Crucita is shown on a *banco* against the plain adobe walls of Sharp's studio; her muted coloring blends well with the light, impressionistically colored brushwork of the background. Sharp's subtle handling of this subject portrays a young woman lost in reverie, perhaps dreaming of her approaching marriage, or of her *Wedding Dress*, the alternate title the artist assigned to the picture.

Joseph Sharp
Crucita—Taos Indian Girl, 1924
Oil on canvas
16 × 20 in. (40.7 × 50.8 cm.)
Los Angeles Athletic Club Collection

Crucita in Later Life
Courtesy Matilda Hadley and Nettie
(Natividad) Lujan

Sharp, *Crucita*   Houlihan

Sharp portrays *Crucita*, one of his favorite Taos models, in a traditional Pueblo woman's dress and footwear. Wool yarn was employed to embroider the design on this cotton manta, the Spanish term used by the Pueblo to designate a shoulder garment or a dress made from a rectangle of cloth. The woven cotton is wider than it is long, and the deep border is embroidered on the white fabric in both positive (black-on-white) and negative designs. When the black inverted triangles extend into the white body of the garment, a positive (black-on-white) design is achieved. At the center of the dark embroidered area, the light vertical bands and the red shapes create negative design effects. Barely visible in this painting, but very common in Pueblo embroidery on cotton, are the horizontal and diagonal bands, which are also created by a negative light color on a dark field. Black or dark blue embroidery is common, as are red, green, and even yellow. While Pueblo embroidery with cotton thread on a cotton ground dates from about 1400, the use of wool yarn does not occur until after the arrival of the Spaniards.

At the end of the nineteenth century, when a number of artists already were painting at Taos, a dress as elaborate as this one would have been reserved for ceremonial occasions. Quite possibly a garment like this one would have been traded to Taos from another Pueblo. Here, we must assume that it was in Sharp's artifact collection. The shawl beside Crucita is of American or possibly Mexican commercial manufacture.

The painting attempts to convey the stark simplicity of a traditional home in Taos Pueblo. Although the actual site was Sharp's studio, the bare walls and sitting platform suggest the typically unadorned Pueblo dwellings. Photographs of the interiors of such homes attest to this spareness. In contrast to this material simplicity is the rich and complex nonmaterial culture of Pueblo art, philosophy, and religion.

Blumenschein, *Old Man in White*   Trenton

Like many of the early Taos artists, Blumenschein's training stemmed from nineteenth-century academic principles and from the disciplines of illustration, a profession he practiced until 1919 when he moved his family to Taos and devoted himself completely to painting. The impact of the New Mexican landscape and its colorful inhabitants was immediate, releasing him from academic conventions to explore new imagery and styles. He described his reactions and those of his colleagues on their first encounter with Taos: "We all drifted into Taos like skilled hands looking for a good steady job. We found it, as it grew into an urge that pushed us to our limits, a joyous inspiration to produce and give to the deepest extent of each man's own calibre. We lived only to paint. And that is what happened to every artist who passed this way."[1]

For Blumenschein, the New Mexican environment with all its mystical quality and color became a stage for imaginative creations that he invested with symbolic associations. He wanted to express the "full reality of the deeper emotional qualities of life as revealed to him in significant symbols."[2] The Pueblo Indian and the Spanish-American—both in an age of transition in which their cultures were rapidly disappearing—and the picturesque, brilliantly lit landscape became subjects for his many canvases.

Blumenschein was concerned with the hardships and spiritual triumphs of the Indian. His early pictures of Indian life reflect this human understanding in their suggested symbolism and emotional tone, emphasizing the dignity of the "noble" race. At this early stage in his career, Blumenschein uses color hesitantly, while his broad, decorative treatment recalls the formulas and ideas seen in his work as an illustrator. By the early twenties, he had progressed from this semidecorative style to such powerful interpretations as *Superstition* and his portrait of *The Plasterer*, both rendered in delicious color harmonies, tapestry-like textures, rhythmic movement, and a sense of architectural order and design.[3] *Old Man in White* (1917) links Blumenschein's early work and his mature style of painting. "A promise of powerful fulfillment"[4] is revealed in this expertly painted, stongly conceived portrait of an aged Pueblo Indian known as Dr. Bird, or the "medicine man," among the Indians he treated. (His real name was Marcio Martínez and his Tiwa name was Chi'u.)[5] The painting demonstrates the artist's ability to grasp the inner emotional qualities of his subjects with deep human warmth. Here, as in the *The Plasterer*, Blumenschein captures an attitude by portraying his sitter in a posture that suggests a dream state. Among the Taos Indians, this ritual act is seen as a source of omens or explanations of past events. Blumenschein also demonstrates his deep understanding not only of body structure but of body movement that expresses emotion and mood. The artist has achieved this rhythmic movement with sweeping brushstrokes, vibrant colors, and strong contrasts of light and shadow in a well-balanced composition—design elements that characterize his later, more mature style.

Soaring Eagle, as the model is sometimes called, sat for his portrait, which the artist developed first as a small sketch without props or decorative detail-

Ernest Blumenschein
Old Man in White, 1917
Oil on canvas
26 × 26 in. (66.1 × 66.1 cm.)
Los Angeles Athletic Club Collection

ing.[6] A photograph of the posed model in the Blumenschein Collection shows the sitter seated frontally against an adobe wall with his fan and the black pot; he is wrapped in a plain, white cotton blanket and wears jeans, a shirt, and decorated Indian moccasins—a combination that reflects Blumenschein's feeling that the standardized American look was gradually weaning the Indian away from "his dress, his dance, his blanket and his pottery."[7] The sitter's expression and mood are far stronger in Blumenschein's two presentations than in the photograph of the model. In all three the sitter's eyes are almost closed. It is said that Chi'u was blind, and when he died in 1927 he was the oldest man in the Pueblo, approximately 127 years old. Blumenschein has presented a moving portrait of an Indian performing a private ritual act—preserving something of the mystique, beauty, and spirit of his culture—an act that might be symbolized by the evocative, abstract effigy delineated on the wall beside him.[8]

Ernst Ruth, Sr.
Soaring Eagle, ca. 1919
Courtesy Museum of New Mexico
(neg. no. 85753)

47

Soaring Eagle (Marcio Martínez), 1917
Courtesy Blumenschein House, Kit Carson
Memorial Foundation, Taos

Blumenschein, *Old Man in White*   Houlihan

The seated Taos man in this painting is something of a mystery, in behavior rather than identity. His name is Chi'u, or Soaring Eagle. But what is he doing in this scene by Blumenschein? The man's closed eyes and drowsy posture may indicate sleep, and from this I would suggest that he is dreaming. More than those of any other Pueblo, Taos Indians practiced dreaming as a ritual act. The source of this activity may relate to the nearby Plains tribes, and I would suggest that the image above and to the right of the man's hand holding the feather fan is somehow meant to relate to his dream. Among the Taos, dreams are the sources of omens regarding coming events and explanations of events that have already occurred.

As seen here, Chi'u is wearing what appears to be an animal skin robe. The piece is actually made of cotton fabric, decorated by an Indian artist with paintings of horses and riders. A textile like this would more likely be used on the Plains, probably as a tipi liner, than in the Pueblos. A few such pieces, however, are known to have existed among the Pueblo, and the proximity of Taos to the Plains makes the presence of these textiles in the Taos area quite credible. Blumenschein used this painted cotton fabric to simulate an animal skin robe.

The hairstyle, moccasins, and leggings all seem correct for Taos. The pottery vessel is probably of Taos manufacture, too, although a true identification is not possible from this painting. Only a close examination of the clay used in forming this pot would yield its actual identity. The last major prop in this painting is the feather fan held by the model. Again, as is the painted textile, this piece is very reminiscent of Plains culture.

Blumenschein, *Girl in Rose*   Trenton

Indian Girl was Blumenschein's alternate title for *Girl in Rose*, painted in the mid-twenties at the height of the artist's career.[1] This sensitive and beautifully crafted portrait captures the sitter in a moment of rest, full of contemplation and natural in her pose. Her well-sculpted, ample hands, adorned with a large turquoise ring, are crossed over her chest in a position that repeats the sweeping curve of her shoulders and emphasizes the semicircular shape of her body. Typically, the artist has orchestrated color and light to achieve dramatic effects and decorative patterning. Here, in addition, he cleverly controls the light to bring out the model's striking features and highlight her flesh tones. He also employs shadows to emphasize her ample and plastic form; the darkish brown-blue shadow above her head repeats the roundness of the crown. The coal-black hair with bluish highlights, worn in the traditional bun and bangs, also suggests plasticity of form, as does the massing of colors in large areas. In its simplicity of form and volume, this portrait marks a turning point in Blumenschein's career, making a connective link beteen his work of the twenties and that of the thirties and forties.

The model was obviously a favorite of the artist; she appears in several of his paintings, among them this work's companion portrait, *Woman in Blue* of 1926.[2] Blumenschein was fond of certain motifs that he reused imaginatively in several of his pictures, sometimes for their symbolic associations and at other times for decorative effect, such as the painted white Indian textile that appears here and in *Old Man in White*. Like other Taos artists, Blumenschein amassed a collection of artifacts to embellish his imaginative creations of Indian life and ceremonials.

Throughout his career, Blumenschein continuously explored fresh means of expression. His awareness and appreciation of the new art movements of his era, as well as his inventive mind, "led [him] away," as he said, "from the strict religion of the Academics."[3] Confirming this, Howard Cook, another Taos artist, noted the skill with which Blumenschein was able to bridge traditional and contemporary artistic values.

> Because of his awareness of the necessity of strong underlying design structure which suggests a contributing abstract quality, his work forms a connecting link between today and the traditional art of the past. From the static envelope of the past he has succeeded in his purposeful search for richer values of creative form, into the fascinating realms animated by imaginative, complicated rhythms with design asymmetrical or subtly balanced, and color as rich as the earth of old Spanish and Indian civilizations.[4]

Clearly, in its style, this painting shows Blumenschein's involvement with the avant-garde ideas of his time.

Ernest Blumenschein
Girl in Rose, 1926
Oil on canvas
30 × 25 in. (76.2 × 63.5 cm.)
Los Angeles Athletic Club Collection

51

Pueblo Indian Woman, Isleta, New Mexico
Fred K. Hinchman Collection
Southwest Museum

Blumenschein, *Girl in Rose*   Houlihan

In this portrait of a young Puebloan woman, Blumenschein again employs the painted cotton fabric that he used in *Old Man in White*. Although the figures and scenes represented on the textile are too indistinct to allow accurate analysis of the piece, one can say with some certainty that it was an artifact of Plains Indian culture and not made by the Pueblo. The realistic images portrayed on these textiles by male artists were usually the war and hunting exploits of their owners. By contrast, painted images by Plains women were geometric or abstract.

If the woman is seated before a painted textile from the Plains culture area, how can we state with certainty that she is Puebloan? I believe her dress is Anglo and, although her jewelry is Southwest Indian (probably Navajo), her hair style is distinctively Puebloan. At Taos Pueblo this was the preferred style for women: bangs across the forehead and down to the ear lobes with the longer hair pulled to the back of the head and tied.

Jewelry in Pueblo culture was usually the preferred means of holding wealth. Bank accounts or money in the mattress were from another culture. Wealth held in personal adornment—jewelry—can be found among Indian groups throughout the Southwest.

The Indian, the Spanish-American, the adobe architecture of the village and Pueblo of Taos—all captivated Saint Louis-born lithographer Oscar Berninghaus and became the subjects of his realistic and precisely rendered pictures. His first visit to Taos in 1899 changed the course of his life. While traveling on the Denver and Rio Grande Railroad through New Mexico, he became intrigued with stories of the quaint, historic village of Taos and decided to make a side trip there. Later, he remarked, "I started on a twenty-five mile wagon trek over what was comparatively a goat trail. After a hard journey I arrived in Taos late in the afternoon, the sun casting its glowing color over the hills that gave the Sangre de Cristo mountains their name. . . . I stayed here but a week, became infected with the Taos germ and promised myself a longer stay the following year."[1] The artist kept his word, returning yearly and finally settling there permanently in 1925. It was during his initial visit, however, that Berninghaus decided to become a painter. To prepare for this challenge, he began studying the fundamentals of composition and design, supplementing his self-training with night courses at Washington University's School of Fine Arts.

In New Mexico, Berninghaus discovered endless subject matter for his portrayals of Pueblo Indian life, which he depicted in a straightforward yet insightful manner. At times the artist "catered to the sheer picturesque, but generally his paintings avoided this common failing."[2] He instead sought to discover and reveal the true essence of native life in Taos in the early twentieth century. To do so, he subtly composed his pictorial elements to show symbolically the impact of the white man's beliefs and ways on traditional Indian life. In *Peace and Plenty*, for example, he illustrates an aged chief, bent and thin, immersed in reverie, perhaps a dream of battle triumphs.[3] Santiago Bernal, second chief of the Big Earring People, posed for many of Berninghaus's paintings of Indian life, including *October—Taos* ("Indian with Pumpkin") and *Santiago—The War Chief*. Bernal's distinctive facial features, aged character lines, stooped posture, and particularly his "quiet-stoic nature" appealed to the artist. Many years after the Indian's death, Berninghaus wrote of the man who had been his lifelong friend.

> Santiago Bernal . . . represents a generation of which there now are but a very few—if any. He was a stately, dignified, venerable old man who carried on the cultural traditions of his people as only he knew it [*sic*]. . . .
>
> I always knew him as a hard and industrious worker in the fields, tended faithfully to his crops and also to his pagan religion—attributes that call for high regard and respect from his people. In later years he was one of the war chiefs whose duty it is to marshall the forces of the men and over see [*sic*] and carry out the activities peculiar to the life of the Pueblo. . . .

Oscar Berninghaus
*One of the Old Men of
the Pueblo*, ca. 1927
Oil on canvas
30 × 36 in. (76.2 × 91.5 cm.)
Los Angeles Athletic Club Collection

He was a bachelor . . . rather unusual in the
Pueblo. . . . While he could not tell his age—there being
no record—I gather from questioning him that he was in
his Eighties when he died."[4]

When free from tilling his crops, Bernal posed not only for Berninghaus but for
other Taos artists. He was a "very satisfying and understanding model," according to the artist. "Between times he would come to the studio frequently and
sit for hours . . . very few words would be exchanged between us—silence
was quite well understood." Unlike the other models Berninghaus employed,
Bernal did not serve as domestic help.

In composing his pictures, Berninghaus placed his model outdoors, preferring to sketch his impressions on the site, a procedure he followed in this
work. He then developed his canvases in the studio. The composition was

Berninghaus in His Taos Studio, ca. 1927
Courtesy Museum of New Mexico
(neg. no. 40393)

Santiago Bernal
Courtesy Julie Montoya, Taos

usually sketched in charcoal, then blocked in with a very thin, even watery, oil, usually blue. For details, he employed his maulstick at the easel. By this method, described in his writing, he was able to achieve the precise detail and painterly effects seen here.[5] *One of the Old Men of the Pueblo* was painted about 1926 and has been exhibited widely in major museum shows.

At the height of his career in the 1920s, Berninghaus constructed a group of major canvases of daily Indian life. In these pictures his models are usually placed prominently in the foreground against a colorful and descriptive background generally related to a theme or an idea he wished to convey in the work. The titles of the paintings often reinforce these ideas. Although there is little fantasy or romanticism in his pictures (most of his material is drawn directly from daily observation of Pueblo life), they are not merely objective statements; each also conveys a symbolic meaning. Later in his career, beginning in the mid-thirties, Berninghaus focused his attention on the New Mexican landscape, experimenting with the interrelationships between the brilliant light and vivid colors, while his figures and animals receded to the middle ground. At this stage he recognized that his work had not kept pace with the times, and therefore he made the necessary changes in his approach and style.

A comparison of Berninghaus's early commissioned series of historic paintings for the Anheuser-Busch Brewery—illustrating epochal events from the opening of the American West—with his series of major works of the 1920s shows a marked improvement in skill. His vigorous brushstroke, vivid colors, and strong compositional design could have been inspired by the works of his fellow Taos artist Ernest Blumenschein. Post-Impressionistic techniques and palette and the sinuous, sweeping line of Art Nouveau can be observed in the paintings of this period by both artists, although each has his own distinctive style and expression.

The model's posture, stance, and in particular his stoic expression and folded hands are subtleties that give significant insight and meaning to his realistic paintings. They suggest that Berninghaus chose to represent Santiago Bernal here in his role as a celibate and priest in contrast to that of a farmer as in *October—Taos* ("Indian with Pumpkin"). As one writer observed, "Berninghaus' art . . . conceals a true psychological understanding of [and sensitivity to] his major subject, the Pueblo Indians."[6]

Berninghaus, *One of the Old Men*   Houlihan

Berninghaus's primary model for this painting is Santiago Bernal, the secondary "chief" of one of the three kiva societies on the north side of the Pueblo near North House. We know, however, that Bernal lived in South House as a bachelor and is reported in Parsons (1936) as being celibate, although the connections, if any, between these few known features of his life are unclear.

The three kiva societies on the north side of the Pueblo are those belonging to the Day People, the Moon People, and the Big Earring People. As second chief of the Big Earring People, Bernal assisted the head of his kiva, a man whose title is generally translated as Big Earring Man. Both men served in these offices for life, and both inherited their positions from their fathers. In the mid-1920s the leader of the Big Earring People is reported to have had the responsibility for organizing the rituals for the Saint's Day, the Deer Dance, and the Buffalo Dance.

The silver earring that Bernal wears may be seen as personal adornment as well as a symbol of the communal body whose spiritual welfare is his primary concern. Among the possessions the Big Earring Man holds in trust are the kiva society's ceremonial bundles as well as its fetish. These of course are

Charles F. Lummis
Taos and Its Threshing Floors
Southwest Museum Collection
(neg. no. 24082)

Charles F. Lummis
Alberto Lujan Wearing Traditional
Wrapped Braids of Taos Men, 1926
Southwest Museum Collection
(neg. no. 24087)

not shown, nor perhaps were even known by the artist; but Santiago Bernal would be expected to succeed the Big Earring Man should he die, and Bernal's knowledge of kiva ritual would be equal to that of his chief.

Both figures in this painting appear in the traditional white blanket. The primary figure also wears his hair in wrapped braids, and one can just discern the bun at the back of the neck that holds the rest of his long hair. It is difficult to state with any certainty the origin (native or commercial) of the other two textiles hanging to the left and right of the old man. It would appear that the artist has placed his model on one of the upper levels of the North House or South House, and some of the vertical poles extending above the roof lines may be ladders. The peeled logs that have weathered gray white are probably pine from trees taken from the nearby forested slopes. Their extensive use in Taos house construction continues today.

Berninghaus has used the Pueblo's drying racks to bring forward the nearly parallel contours of the more distant mountains. The yellow-gold color suggests alfalfa, wheat-straw, or even corn stalks, which were used as stored fodder. Today these storage racks are found scattered throughout Taos Pueblo, in and around both North and South House, although their present locations may differ from those of earlier years. They are used to dry various crops, and in the past they also were used to store animal fodder safely out of reach. The racks consist of four or more upright posts supporting a platform of horizontal logs. With air passing under and over the raised structure, foodstuffs were easily dried. Among the domesticated animals fed from such stores were cattle, horses, donkeys, pigs, and possibly even oxen. The use of mechanical equipment—tractors and trucks—as well as a reduced animal population at the Pueblo, have combined to lessen the number and importance of such racks today. Here, however, the man at the center right edge of the painting is guiding a donkey loaded with firewood. Such was Taos transport in earlier times.

Charles F. Lummis
South House, Taos Pueblo,
with Drying Racks
Southwest Museum Collection

The first artist to win a landmark victory for the Taos Society of Artists was Walter Ufer, who captured the coveted prize at the Carnegie Institute International Exhibition in 1920 for his painting *Suzanna and Her Sisters*. Formally trained at academies in Dresden and Munich, Ufer worked as a commercial illustrator and lithographer in Chicago before coming to Taos in 1914 under the patronage of Carter Harrison, a former mayor of Chicago. The myriad colors, fantastic forms, lucid ethereal light, and picturesque inhabitants of this remote desert country touched Ufer's sensibilities and prompted him to become a painter. His changes from the dark Munich-school tonalities to a lighter palette and more vigorous brushwork were undoubtedly inspired by the unique qualities of this new environment.

Like other Taos artists, Ufer realized that the traditions of the American Indian were fast disappearing under the pressure of "Americanization." "The Indian has lost his race pride. . . . He wants only to be American. Our civilization has terrific power. We don't feel it, but that man out there in the mountains feels it, and he can not cope with such pressure. . . ."[1] Because of his active social conscience and his interest in human values and conditions, Ufer chose to paint the Indian as he saw him: "In the garden digging—in the field working—riding among the sage—meeting his woman in the desert—angling for trout—in meditation."[2] In so doing, he brought into focus the final transition of the Indian society, its alterations and its alienation from the white man's world. In these otherwise realistic portrayals Ufer was subtly depicting the waning dynamics of their culture. The Indian model here is posed as a moccasin mender against the rough-textured background of unsmoothed adobe walls and broken boards; the cracked pot and the acculturation of the model's clothing further reinforce Ufer's social message and concern for the Indian's plight. He understood and sympathized with the Indian's resentment toward the white man who, as Ufer said, "exploited their romantic appearances and sensationalized their ceremonials."[3] He felt the Indian had been unjustly treated as a "curiosity." During his lifetime Ufer actively championed the Indian's cause, and because of his somewhat radical actions he was often subjected to criticism.

The dynamics of Ufer's composition here can be observed in the manipulation of the vigorous brushwork, the vibrant orchestration of colors, and the strong play of light and shadow. The raking sunlight of a late afternoon emphasizes the diagonal thrust of the asymmetrically placed sitter, highlighting the rough walls and a portion of the figure while leaving the rest in deep shadows. The subtle positioning of the model's foot braced against the doorway adds inner tension to a seemingly static and symmetrically composed picture. Although Ufer's general temperament was irascible, his approach to his art was disciplined. He constructed his forms with unerring technical facility and anatomical perfection. An example here is the furrowed brow of the Indian intensely preoccupied with his chore.

It is said that Ufer composed his elaborate pictures in plein air and that he

Walter Ufer
The Red Moccasins, 1917
Oil on canvas
30 × 30 in. (76.2 × 76.2 cm.)
Los Angeles Athletic Club Collection

Ufer at Work in the Field, ca. 1927
Courtesy Museum of New Mexico
(neg. no. 17011)

never made preliminary sketches. He believed that all his energies and vitality should be put into a single, original painting. "Studio work," he said, "dulls the mind and the artist's palette." He wanted the spontaneity and "strength" of the small sketch for his large pictures.[4] After selecting his motif, he brought his model to it. "He [then] drew in his subjects with a medium hard drawing pencil . . . [and] then went over the pencil lines with a permanent blue and turpentine mixed to the easy consistency of a thick ink. Shadows were solidly laid in with this mixture. When the paint dried, he erased all the . . . lines to make a 'cleaner canvas'. . . ."[5] Working in this manner, Ufer thus abandoned the academic principles he learned in Munich.

Like his Eastern Seaboard contemporaries, among them Robert Henri, whom he admired, Ufer embraced realism as a style that provided "a new approach to human and social concerns."[6] Both artists were reacting to the mawkish and sentimental genre paintings of a previous era. Instead of the New York tenements and city dwellers painted by "the Eight," Ufer chose the Indian as his subject and sincerely believed that the beauty of the tricultural Southwest would provide a truly national art for America. His saw his paintings, like *The Red Moccasins*, as the beginning of a new art form for America.

Seated in a doorway bathed in sunlight, this man holding a moccasin can be identified as Taos Pueblo by his hairstyle as well as the white blanket bunched about his waist.

The painting's title, *The Red Moccasins*, may refer to the Taos practice of dyeing the entire upper portion of the men's moccasins. As is the footwear of the Taos women, the men's moccasins are made of two pieces, a soft tanned deerhide upper section and a hard rawhide sole. It is difficult to determine whether the man is wearing moccasins, heelless shoes, or boots that have been altered to conform to the traditional Taos prohibition against heeled footwear within the Pueblo walls. It would seem appropriate to speculate that for the Pueblo people the sharp-angled footwear of Anglos would cut or otherwise harm the earth, which is sacred.

The pottery vessel shown in this painting is probably a ceramic type technically known as Santa Clara blackware. The principal vessel forms are globular jars and flat-bottomed bowls; both forms have flaring rims. These rims are often scalloped, and the undulating rim form is clearly present in the vessel here. Though named after Santa Clara Pueblo, this pottery was also made at San Ildefonso and to a lesser extent at San Juan and Tesuque Pueblos. It is impossible to say where this particular vessel was made inasmuch as there was extensive trading among the northern pueblos. Ufer in all likelihood included the vessel for his own purposes. The pot, however, was almost certainly not made in Taos Pueblo.

The black surface color of this ware is achieved by firing the vessels in a reducing atmosphere. In such a fire, pottery is hardened by baking. About halfway through the firing, fresh air is excluded from the surface of the vessel, usually by smothering the pot with finely ground animal manure. Such a process is sometimes mistakenly referred to as smudging. The difference between

Men's Moccasins
Pueblo
l: 9 in; h: 6½ in.
(22.9 cm.; 16.6 cm.)
Southwest Museum Collection

smudging and reduction firing is that in the latter a chemical change occurs on the vessel surface. Smudging takes place when carbon affixes itself to the vessel surface, and the dark coating can often be removed by wiping the vessel with a rag. To alter the characteristic black surface of the pot shown here, the vessel would have to be refired in an oxidizing atmosphere.

Although it is impossible to specify the pueblo at which this picture was painted, if we assume the man to be a Puebloan, he is clearly a Taos Indian, identifiable by his wrap-braided hair style. Among the Pueblos such a hair style was confined almost exclusively to Taos, the northernmost of the pueblos. The wrapped or braided hair style was borrowed from the Plains tribes, possibly from the Utes or Comanches, with whom the Taos had extensive trade contact. Not visible is the tied bundle of hair at the back of the head.

It is easy to be confused by the man's white garment. It is, in fact, probably two garments; one is a white shirt not unlike those worn by Anglo or Hispanic men of the time, and the second is a white blanket rolled and tied about the waist. The blanket is discernible only by a careful examination of the folds and draping painted by Ufer. Taos men often wore a blanket bunched about the waist. (Other paintings in this exhibition display distinct Taos modes of blanket wearing.)

The importance of heelless boots, shoes, or moccasins to the Taos man is in his adherence to Taos traditions, and the value of such footwear was often impressed on the young by their elders. Although on one level the painting can be viewed as a scene of everyday life in the Pueblo as seen by Ufer, on another level the artist may be making a statement about cultural continuity. Thus the picture may reflect the urging by Taos elders of the young to preserve their traditions.

Jar
San Ildefonso Pueblo
h: 8 in.
(20.3 cm.)
Southwest Museum Collection

67

Mabel Dodge Luhan, whose indomitable force pervaded the cultural and artistic life of Taos in the first decades of the twentieth century, considered Victor Higgins one of the more progressive and forward-thinking of the early Taos artists. The special relationship that existed between the two friends and neighbors (Victor purchased his first house in Taos from her) can be seen in Luhan's choice to reproduce his painting *Daisy Mirabal* on the jacket cover of her book *Taos and Its Artists*.[1] The painting, in one of Higgins's more advanced styles, evolved out of the artist's experimentations with dynamic symmetry in the late twenties and early thirties.[2]

Although Higgins studied in Europe from 1910 to 1914—during the time of the aesthetic revolution on the continent—his early work reflects late nineteenth-century academic principles, particularly his European subjects with their muted palettes and naturalistic pictorial imagery.[3] His immediate response to the New Mexican land and its inhabitants, first experienced on a trip sponsored by his patron Carter Harrison, helped to lift his work above the realm of mere storytelling. As one of the most experimental members of the Taos Society of Artists, with a strong sense of design and color, Higgins simplified his forms and gave them greater volume than in previous pictures. At the same time his brush became more vigorous and his muted palette gave way to vivid color. From 1922 to 1937 he experimented with a new theme—the Indian model in the studio, usually seated and dressed in modified traditional Taos costume.[4] *Sleeping Model*, for example, an early work from this series of paintings, manifests some of the changes taking place in Higgins's style; it prefigures the later, more complicated rational design schemes characteristic of *Daisy Mirabal*, executed about 1931-32. In *Daisy Mirabal*, the artist has liberally employed Cézannesque devices such as the tilted planes of the rug and floor and the repressed foreground plane. Later paintings in the model series, like *Daisy Mirabal*, are also characterized by boldly outlined forms silhouetted against feathery textured backgrounds, again recalling Cézanne. The setting and the positioning of the detached, monumental centered figure are governed by a mathematical system of composition based on the relationship of the diagonal to the sides of a rectangle. Like other artists of the twenties, including Bellows and Henri, Higgins was influenced by Jay Hambidge's interpretation of dynamic symmetry—a pseudoscientific system of ancient origin that offered "fundamental principles, rules, and laws that would be as foolproof as mathematics." Higgins said that his "informal conversations with Henri, Bellows, Hambidge . . . opened up a range of knowledge in the direction of rationalized painting which, even when scientific or quasi-scientific, was plastic enough to offer innumerable occasions for individual research and expression. For the first time I was able to see the spirit or movement which gave, let us say, the Primitives their character. . . ."[5] Higgins believed that "the true modern [not one that distorts], *builds* his picture, he does not merely paint it. He has his superstructure, his foundation, just as an architect has for his buildings [based on mathematics]."[6] In a sense, Higgins was joining other

Victor Higgins
Daisy Mirabal, 1931
Oil on canvas
39 × 24 in. (99.1 × 61 cm.)
Los Angeles Athletic Club Collection

American artists of his time who were exploring modern ideas but also attempting to establish immutable principles of composition based on quasi-scientific methods such as dynamic symmetry. Higgins had moved from a romantic-realistic style of painting into the modern era while exploring new forms and ideas, though he never completely freed himself from representational art.

In *Daisy Mirabal* the centered figure becomes an integral part of the complicated scheme of design, which is further enhanced by the linear patterning of Indian rugs draped around the model and over the chair. Here, the artist "transcends mere representation to arrive at the true essence or spirit of

Roselea "Daisy" Mirabal and Child
Courtesy Mrs. Daisy Quirino Romero, Taos

his subject."[7] Through the feathery brushstrokes of the background, one can observe the faint pencil lines of his geometrical "superstructure," and the painted rectangles on either side of the figures are part of this mathematical design scheme. The frontally positioned model is composed as a pyramidal form based on a series of parallel diagonals. Perhaps, as a reviewer noted, the architecturally built-up form symbolically recalled the "Indian pyramids of the pre-historic Southwest."[8] The outlining, the tilted rug, and the repressed foreground plane are all part of the new ideas Higgins explored in the twenties and thirties.

In reducing his forms to the essential structure in order to realize, as he said, "the spirit—or the movement—or the rhythm" in life, Higgins did not lose sight of painterly effects.[9] He was essentially a painter's painter: the colors, forms, designs, and sweeping brushwork in works like *Daisy Mirabal* were part of a new artistic sureness critically acclaimed in reviews of his exhibitions of the thirties. Higgins had stripped away the inessential to arrive at the essence and was now painting for art's sake rather than merely capturing images in nature.

George L. Beam, *Higgins with Model for* Indian Girl with Parrot
Courtesy Denver Public Library, Western History Department

Higgins, *Daisy Mirabal*   Houlihan

Higgins's painting of Daisy Mirabal offers the viewer an excellent portrait of the Taos woman's costume. Two time periods are represented: the full-skirted belted dress and the colorful shawl are products of later American manufacture, whereas her boots and hairstyle represent traditional Taos.

The folded boots worn by the woman are unique to Taos Pueblo. As is the footwear of the men, the Taos woman's boot is hardsoled. The distinctively folded upper portions may have been inspired by the Spanish boot form of the eighteenth century, or it may have been modeled after the high, tight-fitting Chiricahua Apache boot. Still another possible origin is the combined moccasin-legging of the Plains Kiowa, with whom the Taos had considerable contact. The use of such footwear was traditionally restricted to married and/or older women, as was the hair worn in bangs on the forehead. Because of their bulky folds, the boots necessitated what can best be described as a waddling gait. These boots are constructed of soft deerskin and rawhide, and their upper portion is whitened with white clay or kaolin. Traditionally they were made by men for their women. The folded condition of the boots is usual; however, when they were used for riding horseback, the boots were unfolded to reach high on the thighs to protect the rider's legs. The number of folds varies from two to five.

Of the three textiles in this painting, it seems likely that the more complex rug and the shawl worn by the model are commercial pieces woven by machine, whereas the textile over the chair, with its relatively simple banded designs, may well have been handwoven by an Indian or Hispanic weaver.

Woman's Moccasin
Taos Pueblo
l. overall: 62 in.
(157.5 cm.)
Southwest Museum Collection

Textile
Chimayo, New Mexico
100 × 41 in.
(250.4 × 104.2 cm.)
Southwest Museum Collection

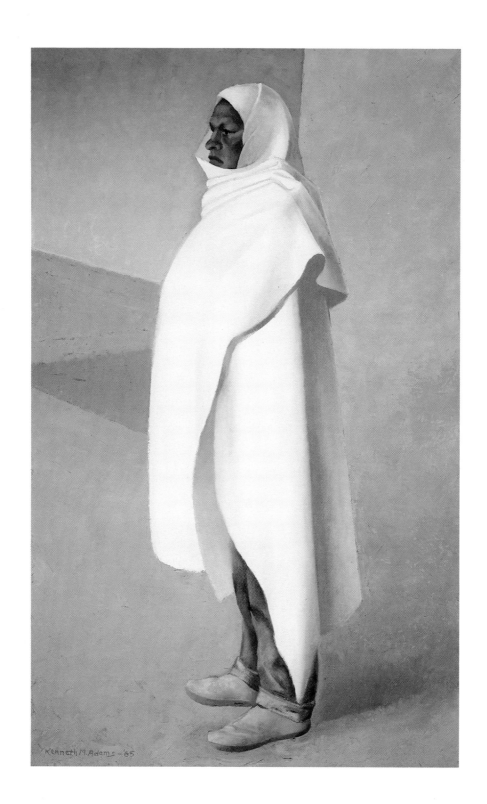

Adams, *Taos Indian*   Trenton

In 1919, while studying at the Art Students League in New York under Kenneth Hays Miller and George Bridgeman, Adams became aware of Andrew Dasburg's work and enrolled in his summer classes at the League's school in Woodstock, New York. Through this French-American teacher Adams learned of the aesthetic principles of Cézanne and the Cubists as well as of the small art community of Taos, where Dasburg had spent part of each year painting since 1918. In 1924 Adams, armed with a letter of introduction to Walter Ufer from Dasburg, became a resident of Taos. Three years later, in 1927, he became the youngest member of the Taos Society of Artists, the year the group disbanded.[1]

From his arrival in Taos, Adams's work had stood apart from that of the Society's other artist-members, whose striking canvases explored the picturesque possibilities of the village in a decorative style. Although trained in the basic tenets of realism, Adams simplified his forms to create strong, basic, abstract designs. He was interested in capturing a "living experience," such as the "haunting face of long-suffering" in his portrait of the Spanish-American *Benerisa Tafoya*, "more than the literary content." He believed that the "candor" of works by Mexican muralists like Diego Rivera and José Clemente Orozco would cause their work to "remain the most socially significant art of the 20th century."[2] Adams shared their compassion for the common man and his condition, as can be seen in his portrayals of his Spanish-American and Indian friends and neighbors. His works share stylistic similarities with some of these muralists as well: the broad treatment of color and shape, the reduction of natural forms to their geometric equivalents, and the precise but exaggerated contours of forms.

Adams frequently used and reused the same subject, "exploring its possibilities in lithography, oil, and watercolor over a period of years."[3] Yet each version was complete within itself, because he continually arranged and rearranged the elements to that end. The bold draftsmanship Adams developed under the tutelage of Kenneth Hayes Miller at the Art Students League continued to be the basis for his controlled and precise definition of form. This facility is equally evident in his drawings and lithographs, which often became the basis for later, finished paintings like *Taos Indian—Evening*.[4] In the lithographic version, the standing *Taos Indian* is also represented in profile, but the blanket is correctly wrapped over the right shoulder instead of over the left as in the painting.[5] Missing in the drawing is the adobe structure, which emphasizes in its abstraction the monumentality and basic sobriety of the Taos Indian.

Adams usually limited the number of colors in his paintings, believing it was "essential to establish the basic color of the largest spatial areas."[6] As his work progressed, he would add colors to his palette only as needed. "It seems to me axiomatic," he said, "that the fewer pigments one uses the greater the command one should have over them."[7] In this painting, Adams has chosen the sandy mud tone of the adobe as his basic color; it acts as a backdrop for the surreal blue sky, blue jeans, and pure white blanket from which the dark, stoic

Kenneth Adams
Taos Indian—Evening, 1965
Oil on canvas
40 × 25 in. (101.1 × 63.5 cm.)
Los Angeles Athletic Club Collection

75

face emerges. All is tinged in the soft pinkish glow of the setting sun. The stark quality of the colors and the interrelationship of masses emphasize the monumentality of the Indian's statuesque pose. In his direct, simple arrangement of forms and color harmonies, Adams has captured the strength and dignity of his subject.

Adams in His Taos Studio, ca. 1927
Courtesy Museum of New Mexico
(neg. no. 40402)

Against the massive Taos masonry, the Indian featured in this Kenneth Adams painting wears the white blanket of Taos. These blankets are commercially made of cotton or flannel and are purchased by the Taos from nearby Anglo or Hispanic merchants. The blanket is worn by the men of Taos Pueblo over the shoulder or bunched around the waist as a kind of kilt. In the past, Taos men wore native moccasins or heelless shoes. Heeled shoes were considered non-Indian and could not be worn within the pueblo walls. The blue denim trousers also seen here were often modified by cutting out the seat to simulate leggings. In time the blanket, the heelless shoes, and the leggings became identified with a Taos man's allegiances to Pueblo tradition.

The walls of the pueblo itself have been used to help define the spatial arrangement within the painting, with an emphasis on mass and color. The fact that the man appears to be standing on adobe indicates that he is portrayed by Adams on an upper level of North House or South House. Although most of the structures are only two-storied, several have three stories, a few have four, and one in North House is five stories high. With few exceptions, the upper stories are storehouses. These adobe walls are replastered annually by the women, who smooth the surfaces with their hands.

Although the interior is not shown in the Adams painting, the flooring of the dwelling would probably have been wood and the furniture sparse. Since 1971 the houses outside the old wall at Taos have had electricity, but the Pueblo has resisted its installation within the walls of North House and South House. Outsiders view this resistance to the modern world as calculated to reduce the impact of American culture with its consequent loss of Indian lifeways.

Affectionately known as the "Green Mountain" by his Taos Indian friends and models, because of his rotund shape and the old green sweater he wore daily, Eanger Irving Couse is widely known for his picturesque Indian subjects.[1] Probably the most celebrated member of the Taos Society of Artists, Couse was not only a talented artist but also a successful entrepreneur in the art world. He was very much aware of changing vogues and gauged his own work accordingly. During his lifetime, he produced approximately 1,500 works, some cabinet size for home decoration and others of salon proportions for exhibition. Realizing the importance of contact with the Eastern art world, he maintained a studio in New York until 1929, where he completed large-scale paintings based on summer studies and sketches made in Taos. Today, his prize-winning paintings are in major private and public collections worldwide. His work was exclusively reproduced on Santa Fe Railroad calendars from 1923 to 1938, and at one time, the railroad owned twenty-seven Couse paintings.[2]

Like many other Taos Society members, Couse showed an early proclivity for drawing. In his native Saginaw, Michigan, he was introduced as a youngster to his first Indians—a small settlement of Chippewas located three miles outside of town. He was later to pursue Indian subjects exclusively in his many canvases. Totally fascinated with art, Couse left high school early to pursue formal training at the Art Institute of Chicago in 1882, where for three months he studied drawing from antique casts. The following winter the artist enrolled in New York's prestigious National Academy of Design School, which he attended for several winters, returning to Saginaw each summer to teach. In September 1886, he departed for Paris with classmates Louis Paul Dessar and Alfred Mayer to study at the Académie Julian under Tony Robert Fleury and William Adolphe Bouguereau—the latter his mentor and greatest inspiration. Like Bouguereau, Couse specialized in the human figure, modeling it with the same surety of hand as his French master. His precocious talent and artistic facility were recognized by the Paris Salon when his work was accepted for exhibition in 1888, the first of many of his paintings to be shown there annually. In Paris he met another art student, Virginia Walker, whose home was on a large cattle ranch near the Columbia River in Washington; he married her in 1889. The following year they returned to the States and settled in Portland, Oregon, where the artist began a long career painting the Indian—this time the Northwest Coast Indians, the Klikitats (Couse's manner of painting in his "Klikitat" period is very different from that of his Taos works—brownish coloring, scumbles and glazes of the pigment characterize the earlier period.)[3] In 1891 the Couses returned to Paris and in 1893 traveled to Etaples, a French fishing village on the English Channel, where Couse painted French peasants, a popular subject for many Americans at the time. In an interview, the artist once mentioned that his peasant subjects sold better than his Indian pictures when he first returned home in the late 1890s, but that he kept on doing Indians for his own amusement. In 1907 his first exhibition of Indian subjects launched

E. Irving Couse
Indian Blanket Seller
Oil on canvas
46 × 34½ in. (116.9 × 87.7 cm.)
Los Angeles Athletic Club Collection

his efforts in this direction.[4]

Couse and his family made their first visit to Taos in 1902 at the recommendation of Joseph Sharp and Ernest Blumenschein, whom he had met in Paris when all three were students. This marked the beginning of the artist's long love affair with Taos and its colorful people. His wife remarked in a letter to her sister that Couse found these Indians more cooperative in posing than the Northwest Coast tribes, who were superstitious about it. She further noted, "The Pueblo is one of the finest in the Country they say and these indians [*sic*] are the very finest types of Pueblo indians [*sic*]—the women can't compare with our northern squaws—they are all short and fat but the men are over six feet, some of them simply fine and they pose without their clothes, just the breech cloth as . . . Couse likes to paint them. . . . He has two of the finest models among them posing for him."[5] (One of them, Big John Concha, might be the model for this painting.) Like his teacher Bouguereau, Couse preferred his models to be scantily clad so that he could record their smooth flesh, tense muscles, and fine bone structure, applying the academic principles he had acquired in Paris. It was obvious to the artist on this first visit that he had found the ideal type of Indian for his paintings—their peaceful ways, willingness to pose, and handsome features were all qualities he desired in his subjects.

Although Couse frequently treated his models as idealized stereotypes, his facile skill as a draftsman and colorist lifts his work above mundane sentimentality. In the Couse memorabilia are thousands of photographs taken by the artist of his subjects and of posed scenes in the studio and in plein air. Many

Couse in His Taos Studio [model Jerry Mirabal], ca. 1910
Courtesy Couse Family Archives, Tucson

80

of them show carefully constructed grid lines across the picture, indicating that the artist transferred these images directly to the canvas for painting—an academic technique of long standing (see photograph).[6] His vignettes of Indian life are characterized by the use of dramatic sidelighting from an open doorway or firelight on the hearth, which adds a romantic and mystical effect to otherwise mundane domestic subjects. Although Couse was steeped in ethnology and could accurately reproduce an authentic event, such as *Moki Snake Dance*, painted after a visit to Walpi in 1903, he preferred instead to present images of "the Indian living a life of idyllic peace" with nature in a preindustrial age.[7] One writer notes, "Couse, like Phillips, was fundamentally a romantic and his paintings were idealizations of the beauty and equanimity of the Indian people. Couse's work extolled what he saw as the purity of primitive life as lived in harmony with the laws of nature."[8] This idealized, noble hero accepting his fate with good spirits and stoical resignation can be seen in Couse's *The Blanket Seller*. Here, a Taos Indian dressed as a Plains warrior assumes the demeaning role of blanket vendor. The striking monumentality of his frontal pose, atypical of Couse's assumed Indian postures, captures our attention with its solid construction and vivid coloring. We are drawn to the haunting eyes of this pleading seller. Perhaps Couse was prophetically telling his audience that the Indian was trying hard to keep his "racial poetry" while bending to the white man's ways. *The Blanket Seller* seems to be an early work, judging from the more distinctive facial features shown here, in comparison with Couse's later works in which idealized and generalized features create a more harmonious whole. Despite criticisms of his sentimentality and his romantic images, Couse was an exceedingly fine artist; his academic training prepared him well to construct pictures that combine carefully posed subjects and aesthetically or thematically related artifacts.

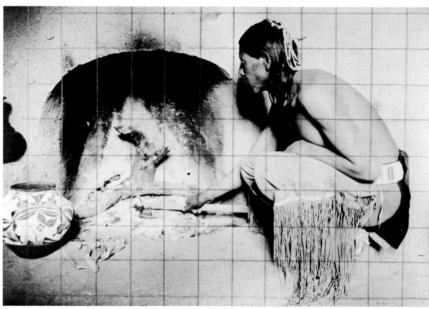

Jerry Mirabal Posing for Couse
Courtesy Couse Family Archives, Tucson

Couse, *Blanket Seller*   Houlihan

Without definitive evidence to the contrary, it seems likely that the man in this painting by Couse is from the southern Plains culture area. This seems probable for four reasons. The hair, although braided, is not the wrapped-braid style of Taos Pueblo; and Taos Pueblo is the only Pueblo in which men regularly and traditionally wore their hair in braids. The presence in the man's hair of what appear to be ermine strips also suggests a Plains identity. While buckskin leggings are common to Taos Pueblo menswear, the suggestion of beadwork above the fringe is indicative of the Plains rather than the Southwest. In fact, the beadwork design suggests Kiowa as the tribal identification. Finally, the bear-claw necklace, although found in many pueblos, is restricted in these societies to religious ritual occasions. It is quite unlikely that an object of such religious importance would be worn casually by a man examining a Navajo textile.

The title of the work, *The Blanket Seller*, suggests one of the problems in determining the identity of the textile. That it is Navajo seems a safe assertion, but whether in fact it is a wearing blanket or a rug is another question. The history of Navajo textiles saw the change in their use from tribal wearing gar-

Bear-Claw Necklace
Unknown Plains Tribe
l. overall: 19 in.
(48.2 cm.)
Collection of Virginia Couse Leavitt

82

Germantown Rug
Navajo
53 × 37 in.
(134.6 × 94 cm.)
Southwest Museum Collection

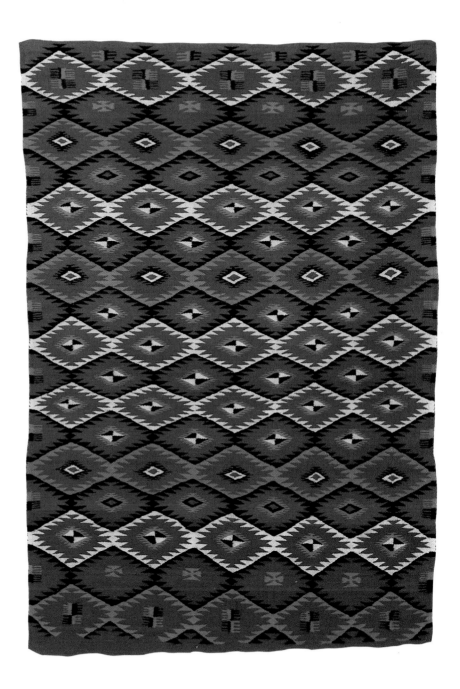

ments or for trade with other Indians to rugs intended as floor coverings. Without examining the actual piece used by the artist, I can only speculate that the piece is a Navajo rug. Yet I believe this to be the case, and based on its design and color I would suggest that it was made of a commercial yarn known a Germantown and that it may date from the 1880s.

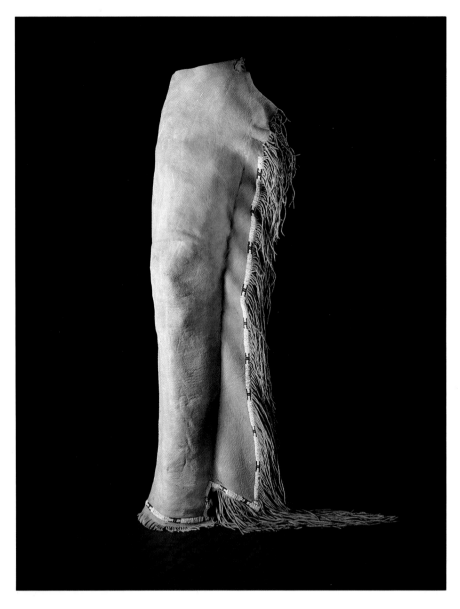

Legging
Taos Pueblo
l: 34 in.
(86.4 cm.)
Collection of Virginia Couse Leavitt

Plains

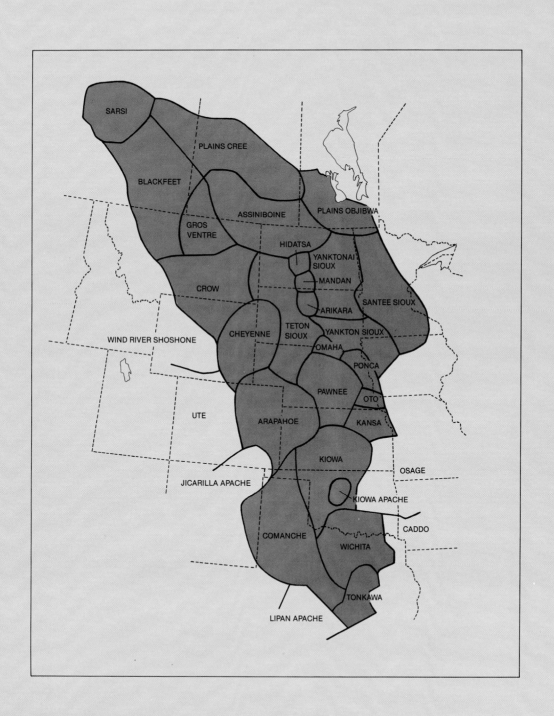

The Great Plains—the vast treeless expanse of grass known to early travelers as the Great American Desert—extends from Canada to Texas and, roughly, from the Mississippi River to the Rocky Mountains. Precipitation is limited: most areas west of 100 degrees longitude receive less than fifteen inches per year. Numerous perennial rivers and streams, however, transect the country from west to east, carrying away the meltwaters of the Rocky Mountain snowpack. The dry regions beween rivers supported hardy and nutritious grasses, such as gamma, bluestem, and buffalo grass, on which great herds of large game animals fed—the elk, the antelope, and most important, the buffalo.

The Plains have been inhabited by humans for thousands of years. The earliest occupants of the area, whose remains have been dated at approximately 8,000 B.C., were hunters of now extinct megafauna, such as the mammoth, mastodon, and giant bison. For about 1,500 years the Plains have been exploited by groups who settled in semipermanent villages along the riverbanks tending gardens of corn, beans, and squash and periodically making forays onto the grasslands to hunt buffalo. The best-known inhabitants of the Plains are the most recent human groups that adapted to the area. With the appearance of European horses on the Plains beginning about 1650 there were new opportunities for exploiting the buffalo herds. Most of the cultural groups commonly associated with the Plains migrated into the area in the seventeenth century—the Sioux, Cheyenne, Crow, Comanche, Arapahoe, and Blackfeet—and their lives were transformed as they took advantage of the bounty offered by horse-mounted buffalo hunting.

This successful cultural adaptation by the Plains hunting societies has captured the imaginations of Europeans for well over a century. These societies of tipi-dwelling, feather-bedecked warriors, once described by an adversary as having "the finest light cavalry in the world," are viewed by anthropologists as amazing examples of rapid cultural transformation in all areas of their lives, from social organization and settlement pattern to sign language. Plains Indian sign language is a remarkable response to an environment of linguistic diversity. Over twenty languages were spoken on the Plains, representing six major language families. In apparent response to the barriers this presented to communication, a complex system of hand signals was developed. Rich in vocabulary, it can convey information, emotions, and even jokes.

There was also an important transition from the lineage- and clan-centered social organization that predominated among the village people to a more flexible, bilateral arrangement in which all members of one's generation might be called brother or sister, an arrangement well suited to a society that had become dependent on an unpredictable resource, like the buffalo. The more widely one could cast his net of kin, the more people he could call on when buffalo were not to be found.

It has been said that to understand Plains Indian societies one must first understand the buffalo. The meaning of buffalo dependence is most clearly reflected in the village organization, or settlement pattern, of the hunting tribes. Buffalo herd size is not uniform throughout the year. Rather, the herds expand and contract in an annual cycle, mirroring the availability of grass. The great land-blackening buffalo herds of travelers' chronicles were an early summer phenomenon, as the animals came together for mating. As the year moved toward winter the buffalo were found in smaller and smaller groups as they spread out in search of forage until, in the dead of winter, they were split into groups of perhaps only a few animals. The settlement pattern of the tribes can be seen as a direct response to the behavior of the buffalo. Tribal encampments for ceremonial and social renewal occurred in the summer and were combined with a highly organized tribal hunt of the large herds. Like the herds, these large villages could not be sustained for long, and soon broke into smaller, more stable groups known as bands. With the onset of winter the bands, in turn, divided into extended family groups that camped in the wooded river bottoms or the mountain foothills until spring allowed the bands to regroup.

Before their culture was interrupted in the late nineteenth century, the Plains Indians were in a process of demographic and political transition. Different tribes not only were spreading onto the Plains and establishing dominance over particular territories but they also were establishing alliances and, in some cases, continuing the process of tribal division that had brought many of the groups to the Plains in the first place. These demographic processes have led to some confusion about cultural affiliations of Plains tribes, often compounded by garbled translations of the group names into European parlance. We find, therefore, politically distinct groups such as the Lakota, Skidi, or Blood placed under more general headings such as Sioux, Pawnee, and Blackfeet. A notable example is that of the Cree Indians living on the Plains of Western Canada, one of whose leaders, Little Bear, was painted by Edgar Paxson. It is important to differentiate the Plains Cree, who moved west from the forested areas of Manitoba and adopted a buffalo-hunting way of life, from the Woodlands Cree, who remained in the lake and forest country, maintaining a dependence on wild-rice gathering combined with hunting and fishing.

The demise of buffalo culture was brought about primarily by disease, military confrontation with the United States Army, and the destruction of the food base, the buffalo. What had once been considered a wasteland, suitable only for Indians, became after the Civil War a region manifestly destined to be encompassed by the continuing expansion of the American frontier. From the beginning the Plains tribes occupying the area were well aware of the threat posed by American encroachment, first by immigrants traveling to Oregon and California, later by the railroads, and eventually by settlers and gold seekers. These tribes opposed the loss of their territories bitterly and often successfully. Not until the buffalo had been depleted to the extent that they were no longer a dependable food source—an act of planned extermination encouraged by federal policy to force the defeat of the tribes—was military resistance overcome. The final military victory by the Plains tribes was the combined action by the Lakota and Cheyenne tribes in June 1876, in which Crook was defeated on Rosebud Creek, and then Custer's command was wiped out on the Little Big Horn. Among the many warriors who achieved honor in the battle with Custer was the Cheyenne leader, Two Moons, whose portrait by Joseph Sharp is included in this exhibition.

CHIEF TWO MOONS  CHEYENNE

Joseph Sharp, *Two Moons*
Sharp Photographic Collection
Courtesy C. M. Russell Museum,
Great Falls, Montana

Joseph Sharp
Chief Two Moons—Cheyenne, 1907
Oil on canvas
12 × 8 in. (30.5 × 20.3 cm.)
Los Angeles Athletic Club Collection

Sharp, *Two Moons*   Trenton

Like George Catlin, the earlier painter of American Indians, Joseph Sharp fully sensed the passing of a vanishing era and the exigencies of making a pictorial record of the Indian and his traditional way of life. Most of his career was dedicated to this objective, and it earned him the laudatory title "the anthropologist" from his fellow Taos Society artists. His facile, academic style of drawing and painting enabled him to reproduce with ethnographic accuracy the distinctive physiognomies and costumes of the various Indian tribes. It was said that because of a hearing disability his eyes were especially keen in perceiving "more in nature, people, and things, than the ordinary individual."[1] In addition, Sharp's passionate understanding of the plight of the Indian allowed him to imbue his reportorial works with a truer feeling for the native American's characteristics, idiosyncrasies, and aspirations. Because of his unique combination of skill and sensitivity, Sharp is considered one of the foremost delineators of the Indian in American art.

Although Sharp's travels took him first to the Southwest, he vowed earlier in his career to record the great warriors or leaders of the Northern Plains before time ran out. He recognized that such men were fast disappearing and their tribal customs rapidly becoming "Americanized." From 1902 to 1910 he divided his time between the Southwest and the Northwest, spending the fall and winter months in a permanent home at the Crow Agency in Montana. In his studio on wheels, Sharp captured likenesses of the various Northern Plains Indians with his camera and brush. In an article, Sharp was quoted as saying, "Though the plains indians [*sic*] are not disinclined to pose, you must never count upon getting a second sitting."[2] His remarks undoubtedly explain why the artist amassed a large collection of photographs and artifacts. Later the same Plains Indian artifacts were to serve as backdrops or costumes for his many paintings of Taoseños.

During the time he spent at the Crow Agency, Sharp painted some 200 portraits of Indians who fought against Custer in the 1876 Battle of the Little Big Horn.[3] In many instances he did several versions of the same Indians, also recording them and others in photographs. The famous Northern Cheyenne warrior *Two Moons*, who led his people against Custer and later served as a scout for the United States government, posed several times for Sharp. Two earlier extant portraits of the physically large and powerful Indian, erect in stature, show him adorned in a red shirt trimmed with ermine tails and a large bear-claw necklace that marked him as a "noted hunter" who had "killed the largest bear of his tribe," according to the artist. Sharp described him as "a heroic figure—an ideal Indian in every physical characteristic with a beautiful and noble character."[4] The artist's close rapport with his subject is evident in all of Sharp's portraits of Two Moons. Although all of them portray the same physical characteristics, their techniques range from the tighter more linear recording of the Lowie Museum of Anthropology, Berkeley, version to the later, more painterly representation in the Los Angeles Athletic Club Collection.[5] When Hamlin Garland wrote of Custer's last battle based on Two Moons's memories of the account, he described the famous warrior-scout.

> There was something placid and powerful in the lines of
> the chief's broad brow, and his gestures were dramatic and
> noble in sweep. His extended arm, his musing eyes, his
> deep voice combined to express a meditative solemnity
> profoundly impressive. There was no anger in his voice,
> and no reminiscent ferocity. All that was strong and fine
> and distinctive in the Cheyenne character came out in the
> old man's talk. He seemed the leader and the thoughtful
> man he really is—patient under injustice, courteous even
> to his enemies.[6]

The qualities Garland saw are evident in this portrait of *Two Moons* painted at Lame Deer, Montana, in 1907, when the Indian, according to the artist, "was almost blind." Glories of past wars lingered on in the old Indian's memories, but Sharp's brush has caught the resignation etched in his face. Relaxed and no longer at war with the white man, Two Moons now simply wanted his people to have a share in the white man's world. In painterly fashion, Sharp's portrait expresses Two Moons's universal ideal.

The Cheyenne Indian, Two Moons, should not be confused with his nephew of the same name. The Two Moons portrayed by Sharp was born about 1847 and played a prominent part in the history of the Northern Cheyennes, until his death in 1917. Initially, as a lesser chief of the Kit Fox Society, one of the oldest Cheyenne military societies and protectors of the ritually important Sacred Arrows, he was an active warrior against the U.S. Army. He is well known for his participation in the 1876 Battle of the Little Big Horn.

By 1877 the military pressure against the Northern Cheyennes resulted in the surrender of Two Moons and his band of followers at Fort Keogh, near present-day Miles City, Montana. After surrendering to General Nelson Miles, Two Moons along with most of his group became scouts for the U.S. Army, and in this new capacity they participated in military actions against other Indians. In 1884 Two Moons and his followers were settled on a reservation near Lame Deer Creek at the Tongue River Agency.

Two Moons lived a relatively long life—seventy years—and was photographed on numerous occasions by the pioneer Montana photographer L. A. Huffman, whose studio was in Miles City. Joseph Henry Sharp also made photographs as well as paintings of the Indian chief.

It was probably Two Moons's facility with English that enabled him to be a frequent spokesman for the Cheyennes. For example, in spring 1913, Two Moons and six other Cheyennes visited Washington and other East Coast cities. Wooden Leg, a member of the contingent, recounts this trip in his autobiography, *A Warrior Who Fought Custer*:

> I went to Washington when I was fifty-five years old. Little Wolf, Two Moons and Black Wolf were old men with me as delegates to speak for our tribe. . . .
>
> Two Moons did most of the talking for us. The rest of us did not care to make any long talks. Two Moons told these people he was a big chief leading all of the Cheyennes at the Custer battle. None of said anything in dispute of him at the meeting, but when we got away to ourselves Black Wolf said to him: "You are the biggest liar in the whole Cheyenne tribe." Two Moons laughed and replied: "I think it is not wrong to tell lies to white people" (Thomas Bailey Marquis, interpreter [Minneapolis: Midwest Co.,1930]).

In Sharp's painting the necklace worn by Two Moons appears to be made of blue glass beads. It is difficult to determine whether these were trade beads or beads made of blue glass melted and shaped by Indians. The technique of melting glass was not widely known, and the process itself was accompanied by a ceremony. Before they had access to glass trade beads, the Cheyennes made colorless beads from the quartz sand found on anthills by melting it in a pottery vessel. Later, they melted the sand in metal ladles used to make lead bullets.

Although Edgar S. Paxson was less flamboyant than his contemporary, the celebrated Western artist Charles Marion Russell, Montanans considered him an important home-state artist who faithfully recorded the territory's frontier history in paintings and drawings. His well-known murals of the Lewis and Clark expedition of 1803-6 in the state capitol and the Missoula County Courthouse attest to his unique talent of combining history with picturemaking. Recognizing Paxson's special role as preserver of Montana's frontier life, Russell wrote an appreciation at the time of the other artist's death: "Paxson has gone, but his pictures will not allow us to forget him. His work tells me that he loved the Old West. . . . The iron heel of civilization has stamped out nations of men, but it has never been able to wipe out pictures, and Paxson was one of the men gifted to make them."[1]

Paxson and Russell arrived in Montana Territory in the late nineteenth century, a transitional period characterized by the "final subjugation of the Indians, [the] end of the buffalo, the change from roaring, wide-open camps to crude cow-towns, [the] beginning of fencing of the vast open range and the last of the Texas trail herds."[2] Their firsthand knowledge of the Indians, mountain men, and settlers was transferred to their canvases in colorful pictorial records of Montana's frontier life and its adventurers. Each attempted to document that dramatic phase of America's history—Charles Russell in his action-packed narratives of the wild West and Edgar Paxson in his carefully researched and delineated scenes from history. Despite their different approaches both artists preserved a measure of Western history for future generations.

Unlike Russell, Paxson—scout, hunter, soldier, and artist—was a quiet, unassuming man of Quaker background and principles. His more stolid and modest nature often was reflected in the subdued character of his work. Even his color was restrained in contrast to Russell's lively, chromatic, run-rampant canvases. Less promotion-minded and perhaps not as sure of his talents (or lacking a champion and promoter like Russell's wife, Nancy), Paxson kept his prices depressed even during the years of his peak sales from 1900 to 1911. New York never became an outlet for his work; Paxson depended on local sales and commissions for his bread and butter. Like Russell, Paxson was self-trained, acquiring his artistic knowledge from firsthand experience of Western life, drawing and painting handbooks, reproductions, and occasional visits to museums and galleries to view European and American paintings. A brief trip to Chicago in 1903 would seem to verify such visits. In his journal the artist singles out the German-American landscapist Albert Bierstadt as a source of inspiration.[3] He mentions that Bierstadt's scenic extravaganza *Laramie Peak* left a lasting impression on him. Although he was very much affected by Bierstadt's work, there is little evidence in Paxson's own pure landscapes or in his scenic backdrops of that influence. It is more likely that Paxson was influenced by the German Late Romantic painters, as were other regional artists of the time. In *Little Bear*, the reddish-tinged, scenic background with its snow-clad

Edgar Paxson
Little Bear, Chief of the Crees, 1912
Oil on canvas
28 × 22 in. (71.1 × 55.9 cm.)
Los Angeles Athletic Club Collection

peak seems to indicate this source of inspiration, particularly in its generalization.

Although the greater portion of Paxson's work was done in the first decades of the twentieth century, his grandson noted that the artist's way of life was more attuned to nineteenth-century philosophy. "The new technological frontier was strange and occasionally unbelievable to him."[4] Caught up in the history of exploration and frontier life, he was an avid reader of history and a researcher as well. His sources included photographs, printed documents, and tales or oral histories by Indians who had engaged in warfare or served as scouts. He enjoyed hunting and fishing, conversing with his pioneer friends, and amassing a large artifact collection. He even took to "wearing his hair long and in the style of Buffalo Bill, with accompanying mustache [sic], goatee and wide brimmed hat."[5] Occasionally, he was seen in town on horseback, wearing a buckskin shirt and leggings and wrapped in an Indian blanket. It is even claimed that he sometimes let out a war whoop. The Indian more than the pioneer became the subject for his many canvases. He had a strong compassion for Indians, who suffered from the changing society. Despite this sympathy, he never took sides, believing that both whites and Indians should be judged as individuals. He condemned the duplicity of the whites but was critical of the atrocities committed by the Indians against the early settlers. His thoughts are found in the margins of the many books in his library. According to his journals and guest book, he had many Indian friends. Among them were Two Moons, who told him stories of the Battle of Little Big Horn, and Louison, Judge of the Flatheads, whose portrait he painted in 1914.[6]

Paxson's acquaintance with Little Bear, Chief of the Crees, dates to 1904, when he is first recorded in the artist's journal and guest book: "Mus-que-sish is down from Canada, he with his interpretor [sic] made a long visite [sic]. he is a large fellow—quite inteligant [sic]. he and 'Sitting Bull' also 'Crow Foot' Chief-of-the-Blackfoot were great friends. he seems well informed on all the late indian wars especially the Little Big Horn fight—and the 'Joseph' rade [sic] of—'77,' he will call again on monday." Little Bear's name, however, does not reappear in Paxson's journal until 1912, when the artist mentions painting a portrait of him for Frank Linderman of Helena, Montana. Linderman was a literary figure and a champion of Indian causes, and he was acting as an agent for the poet and newspaperman John Ritch of Lewistown, who had commissioned the portrait. On 31 October 1912, "the day after Vice President J. S. Sherman died," Paxson completed his portrait of *Little Bear*, noting the finished product with much satisfaction.[7]

Curiously, the revered Little Bear was never portrayed by Russell. According to old-timers' recollections, Russell preferred the dramatic narrative over the portrait for its own sake. This might explain in part why Paxson landed this commission, since Linderman and Russell were close friends, and Russell had illustrated several of the writer's stories. At the time the cowboy artist was busy with shows in New York and his works were commanding sizable sums.

Nowhere in Paxson's journals is there mention that Little Bear actually sat for his portrait. Ritch's daughter, who knew Little Bear when she was a child,

Herbert Titter, *Little Bear*, 1911
Courtesy C. M. Russell Museum,
Great Falls, Montana

states that Herbert Titter's photograph of the Cree chief, taken in Lewistown, Montana, in 1911, served as the model for Paxson's portrait. The same photograph is reproduced in Linderman's book *Indian Old-Man Stories*, accompanying a poem dedicated to Little Bear by the author.[8] The painterly yet modeled effect of this portrait, which contrasts sharply with the more two-dimensional, hard-edged portrait technique seen in his Indian heads taken from life, supports the use of a photographic reference. Although the painting and photograph are quite close, the artist has taken certain license in individualizing his portrayal of this renowned chief. There are slight changes in costume and posture: Little Bear is wrapped in a trade blanket, and his tall wolfskin hat with its eagle coup feather has been cropped; but more important, the artist has included the subject's hand with outstretched thumb pressing the peace medal worn around his neck. The medal, however, is engraved with a different image than the one shown in the photograph of Little Bear, indicating that Paxson might have substituted one from his own collection. It undoubtedly symbolizes Little Bear's role as a peacemaker among men as well as his leadership of a small renegade band of Montana Chippewas and Cana-

Paxson's Butte, Montana, Studio, 1906
Courtesy Underwood Stereoptic Views
Collection of William Paxson, Sr.

96

dian Crees camped outside of Helena in the early twentieth century. With no home, reservation, or place to make a living, they were dependent on humanitarian acts of people like Frank Linderman, who appealed in their behalf and finally got the United States government to set aside land for them and to establish the Rocky Boy Reservation near Havre, Montana. According to Linderman, this was only after their old leaders, such as Little Bear, "had gone to the shadow-hills."[9]

In this portrait, Paxson has captured the fierce pride of the Indian chief: his boring eyes, pierced lips, and lower protruding lip unmistakably show that his resolute character has not escaped the artist. Describing Little Bear, Linderman remarked, "[He] was a born fighting man. His face was like a Roman senator's, and yet lurking in his eyes there was an easily awakened expression of keen humor. He laughed readily, but was decidedly moody, his mouth suggesting a pouter."[10] Paxson manages to soften the portrait somewhat by use of tactile effects: the woolly cloth of the blanket, the soft furry animal hair and skin, and the suffused wintry landscape in the background. It is apparent that the artist wished to establish the Indian's home territory by including a bit of the cold northern Rockies in the background. Paxson has left us a prominent, sensitive, and lasting portrait of Montana's Chief of the Crees.

Paxson, *Little Bear*   Houlihan

Edgar Paxson's painting of Chief Little Bear was most probably based on a photograph by Herbert Titter of Lewistown, Montana. While Little Bear is not wearing a trade blanket, in Titter's photograph the pose as well as the artifact inventory—wolf skin hat, hair ornaments, and peace medal—are the same.

Little Bear was the leader of a combined band of Canadian Cree and Chippewa Indians who lived in Montana. The Chippewa had moved to Montana from Wisconsin and Minnesota about 1860 to hunt buffalo. They remained there and were joined after 1885 by Crees seeking to escape Canadian and British military authorities. The Crees and Chippewas lived together and foraged for food and shelter. By 1916 they were camped outside of Helena where they were befriended by Frank Bird Linderman, a well-known Montana writer and ethnographer. Through the efforts of Linderman, land was set aside and the Rocky Boy Reservation created. At one point the band was referred to as "Linderman's Indians," so numerous were his efforts on their behalf.

It would be difficult to discern the tribal identity of this Paxson portrait if the model were not known. None of the accessories—hat, hair ornaments, trade blanket, peace medal—is specific enough to yield a tribal association closer than northern Plains Indian culture.

Linderman dedicated his second book, *Indian Old-Man Stories*, to "Little Bear, Chief of the Crees," and a short poem to Little Bear appears near the title page. The wolfskin hat along with several other Cree artifacts are presently in the Linderman Collection, which will be given to the University of Montana.

Warren Rollins, who was known as the dean of the Santa Fe art colony, lived to be over 100 years old, nearly fourscore of those years spent working as an artist.[1] Born in Carson, Nevada, in 1861, Rollins was raised in Northern California where he attended the San Francisco Art Association and California School of Design under Director Virgil Williams, from approximately 1882 to 1886. He then served as the school's assistant director until 1887, when he married and moved to Oakland to teach art. His peripatetic nature and fondness for unique subject matter took him on a long pilgrimage that led first to Portland, Oregon, where he taught art courses at the YMCA; then to Southern California, Arizona, Wyoming, and Montana; and finally back to Northern California. There he opened a studio in San Francisco and divided his time between teaching and sketching in order to support his growing family.

Between 1905 and 1906, Rollins made two trips to the Hopi country, where he headquartered at the Hubbell Trading Post in Ganado, Arizona—a popular gathering place for writers and artists (see Leigh entry). Because of his "personal charm and wit," his biographer grandson writes, he soon made friends with the Hopis at Oraibi and "gained the privilege of sketching scenes in the kivas during religious ceremonies."[2] An able draftsman, Rollins produced some carefully drawn anatomical studies of his Indian subjects later translated into the large wall canvases that decorate the dining room walls at Bishop's Lodge outside of Santa Fe. They record the Hopi myths, legends, and ceremonial rites in which the artist became steeped while living among the Indians at Oraibi. His work of that early period is particularly meaningful since the Hopi were already living in an age of transition, experiencing changes in many of their customs and traditions.

During a visit to Arizona in 1909, Rollins met the noted archaeologist-ethnologist J. Walter Fewkes, who was conducting exploratory work in the Southwest. It was undoubtedly Fewkes who urged Rollins to visit the Indian pueblos in northern New Mexico. In late spring of 1910, Rollins and his family traveled to Santa Fe and then to Taos, where they spent most of the summer. At that time, Santa Fe consisted of the Governor's Palace, the plaza and its shops, San Miguel Church across the river, and a small residential area. The artist was favorably received by local officials and society leaders. The latter organized an exhibition of his desert scenes and Indian subjects in the Historic Reception Room of the Old Palace on 7 June—probably at the suggestion of Fewkes, since the show was held under the auspices of the School of American Archaeology.[3] A reporter noted that Rollins, "unlike many artists who painted from the outside and gather their impressions from the windows of a Pullman car, . . . [had] lived among the Indians . . . for several years . . . [and] his paintings [reflected] a faithful picture of their life."[4] The artist's Indian pictures seem to have been the chief attraction; these works, including Rollins's more recent studies of Indians made at Laguna Pueblo, west of Santa Fe, were singled out by the same reporter. This latter bit of information confirms a scholar's observation that the rock formation in Rollins's finished painting *The Historian*,

Warren Rollins
The Historian, 1910
Oil on canvas
40¼ × 28¼ in. (102.3 × 71.3 cm.)
Los Angeles Athletic Club Collection

Elizabeth Chatham, *Rollins Sketching
Outdoors*, ca. 1950
Courtesy Elizabeth Chatham, Santa Fe

based on one of these studies and executed late in 1910 after his return to Southern California, is similar to those found around the Laguna Pueblo area.[5]

After leaving New Mexico the Rollins family traveled to Southern California, where they established a residence in San Gabriel. On 25 September 1910, *Los Angeles Times* critic Antony Anderson reviewed the summer studies brought back from the artist's sketching tour in New Mexico. He reported that Rollins was planning "a series of twelve pictures which would remain a record of the domestic, ceremonial and idyllic life of the Indian of today."[6] He added that the artist hoped to finish the series before the end of the year, having just completed two of the twelve works. "*The Historian* also belongs to this series. The sketch for the picture shows us a young man etching on an adobe wall [*sic*] some thrilling story of his tribe. He is just placing the great sun symbol on the soft sandstone." This sketch was later translated into a painting, which was reproduced in the same newspaper on 12 March, 1911.[7] Whether or not Rollins completed the series remains a mystery today. *The Historian*, like his masterpiece, *Grief* (showing a Zuni Indian mourning his wife), from another series, is mainly a product of the artist's imagination. The Indian in this picture is a composite of types and is somewhat apocryphal, having no real relationship with the Pueblo Indians. The glyph he is carving with a modern tool has been identified as "an elaboration of the sun symbol—its rays and inner circle a product of the artist's invention."[8] Although the setting is based on reality, the picture is largely storytelling. It is evident that the lore and mystique of these ancient people were far more appealing to the artist than the actual scenes he sketched around the pueblos. Rollins was a self-proclaimed realist whose work reflected his academic training. Yet his awareness of modern art movements is noticeable in the light, impressionistically treated background. Interestingly, Rollins produced another version of the same Indian carving a petroglyph of a different design; it is not dated and the title is unknown.[9]

In 1917, Rollins established a studio in Santa Fe, where he spent much of his time until the death of his wife in 1925. Thereafter he wintered in Baltimore with one of his daughters and spent his summers with the other in Chaco Canyon. A series of works he did there were later adapted as illustrations for his granddaughter's book on the history of these famous ruins.[10]

During the thirties Rollins decorated the United States Post Office in Gallup, New Mexico, with murals done under the auspices of the WPA. In later years, after contracting palsy, he took up the art of wax-crayon drawing—quite successfully, judging by reviews of his work.[11] Throughout his long career his work attracted the attention of the Santa Fe Railroad Company, and its collection includes his works today.

In his little black book, in which he jotted down notes and ideas, Rollins expressed his attitude toward art: "I am of the opinion that there is no modern or old art, but there is art only which is as old as man thinks and feels, and will exist as long as man will conceive and create, there is no formula for artistic creation. Art is not a copy of nature, it is in a sense its equivalent."[12] Rollins's art has its place in the scheme of American art: it carries in its visual statement the artist's wish and vision that the history, lore, and myth of the American Indian be carried forth and indelibly imprinted on the minds of future American generations.

Sankawai Canyon
George Wharton James Collection
Southwest Museum

Rollins, *The Historian*   Houlihan

Much of what is portrayed by Rollins in this painting is contradictory. All of the costume elements—blanket, moccasins, hair decorations—suggest a Plains Indian identity for the figure, while the rock art is from the Southwest. The native technique for producing such art, however, does not utilize a hammer and chisel, as seen here. Rather, a hammer stone was used directly against the rock to "peck" out an image. Rock art of this style is probably inspired by the rock art of northern New Mexico. We know that Rollins lived and worked in Santa Fe, and it seems safe to suggest that he may have seen a good deal of rock art around Galisteo or in the northern Rio Grande area. This picture is probably a free improvisation on what he observed there.

WILD HORSE WINNEBAGO. RES.   John Hauser. 1902

Hauser, *Wild Horse*   Trenton

It is not known when or how Cincinnati-born Hauser became interested in painting Indian scenes. His formal art training at the Royal Academy of Fine Arts in Munich under Nicholas Gysis undoubtedly improved his technical proficiency in drawing and composition, but it hardly gave him an opportunity to see or study pictures of American Indians.[1] In 1885 he returned to Europe with fellow Cincinnati-artist Joseph Sharp.[2] Two years earlier they had joined forces in Santa Fe and had traveled by wagon to several New Mexican pueblos including Tesuque and San Juan (not reaching Taos), where they sketched and carefully observed the various Pueblo Indians, their customs and rituals. The experience was probably a high point in the careers of both artists. According to Sharp, "Anyone willing to sacrifice a few modern comforts and rough it through the mountains and indian [*sic*] pueblos of New Mexico can experience a novel life, fully repaying the time and trouble."[3] Perhaps this experience inspired Hauser's lifelong goal to record the different Indian tribes. In 1901 he and his wife, Minnie, were adopted into the Sioux nation. Both received Indian names: Hauser, "Straight White Shield," and Minnie, "Bring Us Sweets."[4]

Unlike his friend Sharp, Hauser chose to remain and work in his native Cincinnati, where he first attended the Ohio Mechanics' Institute and later studied drawing at the McMicken Art School in 1873. For several years he taught drawing in the public schools until his second study trip abroad. Sometime after 1891 he began traveling through the Indian country of Arizona and New Mexico, visiting the Navajo and Apache reservations and later the Pueblo of Taos. It is said that he and Sharp were in Taos together in 1893, purportedly the first visit there for both.[5] Several of Hauser's existing Indian paintings show the Taos Pueblo in the background, although none is dated. Why Hauser did not follow Sharp's example and join the small Taos contingent of artists is a mystery. Since similarities have been noted between Hauser's work and that of Cincinnati's celebrated Indian painter Henry Farny, it might be that Farny's influence on Hauser overshadowed that of the Taos artists. Both Hauser and Farny were equally captivated by the Sioux Indians and produced a number of paintings of them. It appears that both artists preferred working in gouache, and many of their most successful pictures are developed in the lighter medium, even though each produced many oils.

For about two decades, Hauser made yearly visits to the Indian country, undoubtedly to gather material for his studio work. He is known to have created a remarkable series of portraits of notable chiefs, including American Horse, Red Cloud, Sitting Bull, Spotted Tail, High Horse, and Lone Bear.[6] While the title of this painting has been inscribed on the canvas by the artist, the Indian's identity remains problematic. It may be that his colorful costume inspired the work, and Hauser has even included a few pictorial devices, such as the horse and skull, to make the scene more believable and nostalgic. Whatever his iconographic intention, the picture is interesting from an anthropological point of view.

John Hauser
*Wild Horse Winnebago
Res[ervation]*, 1902
Gouache
14 × 10 in. (35.6 × 25.5 cm.)
Los Angeles Athletic Club Collection

Hauser's title for this painting *Wild Horse Winnebago Res[ervation]* is a source of some confusion. The title implies that this is a man named Wild Horse, a Winnebago Indian living on the Winnebago Reservation in northeastern Nebraska, but this probably is not the case. It would have been very unusual to name a Winnebago *Wild Horse* in 1902, the date given to the painting. Winnebago names generally incorporated clan affiliation, and because all of their clan references precede the coming of the horse, Winnebago names do not refer to the horse until much later in this century.

It is possible that the site for this painting was Nebraska, although the landscape could have derived from the artist's memory or possibly from a photograph. The clothing is painted without enough detail to identify its tribal origin or even whether its decorations are of porcupine quills or glass beads. Below the figure's right hand there appears to be a pipe bag, and the hourglass designs seen here suggest Crow Indian origin for the bag. Again, it is possible that Crow artifacts were traded east from Montana, but a more likely explanation is that the pipe bag was the property of the artist.

The rifle is probably of Winchester manufacture and is often called a "yellow boy," its name derived from the brass plate seen just above the figure's right hand. The position in which the rifle is held is very reminiscent of the postures employed by R. A. Rinehart in photographs he made of a large number of Indians who had traveled to Omaha for the Trans-Mississippi Exposition and Indian Congress in 1898.

If this painting was done in northeastern Nebraska, it is more probable that the model was Dakota or Omaha. Of the two the latter seems more likely, because the tribe is native to Nebraska and both hat and neck ornament suggest Omaha. As a tribal group, Omaha may refer to either a single tribe or to a group of five historically related tribes including the Omaha, Osage, Kansa, Ponca, and Quapaw. One of the strongest indications that the figure here is Omaha, or of a related tribe, is the draping of the blanket. In the primary reference source

Rifle
Winchester, 44-caliber, rim fire
l: 43½ in.
(110.6 cm.)
Southwest Museum Collection

on the Omaha there is a series of nine photographs that depict the "language of the robe." The Omaha and their related tribes used the wearing robe to convey information. These photographs reproduce the nine robe positions, or drapings, and their meanings. In the Hauser painting, the robe is worn as an "admonition . . . [suggesting] . . . a pause, a change of attitude. The mind of the speaker has reverted to some past experience in his long career, from which he draws a lesson and gives it as an admonition to the people" (Alice C. Fletcher and Francis LaFlesche, *The Omaha Tribe*, Bureau of American Ethnology, 27th Annual Report, [1905-6], 362).

Admonition, The Language of the Robe Courtesy Alice C. Fletcher and Francis LaFlesche, *The Omaha Tribe*, Bureau of Ethnology, 27th Annual Report (1905-6), pl. 53d.

Preface

1. Ernest L. Blumenschein, "Origin of the Taos Art Colony," *El Palacio* 20 (15 May 1926).
2. Michael Macdonald Mooney, ed., *George Catlin Letters and Notes on the North American Indians* (New York: Clarkson N. Potter, Inc., 1975), 254.

Raschen   *Pomo Interior*

1. For Leigh's letter to his mother of 25 November 1891 about this trip, see D. Duane Cummins, *William Robinson Leigh, Western Artist* (Norman: University of Oklahoma Press and Tulsa: Thomas Gilcrease Institute of American History and Art, 1980), 45; 179, n. 83. See also artist's biographical card with information supplied by Raschen in 1907; all additional data on the artist comes from this source unless otherwise noted.
2. See Pierre N. Boeringer, "Original sketches by San Francisco Painters," *Overland Monthly,* 2d ser., 27 (April 1896): 361-69.

Hudson   *Ka-ma-ko-ya*

1. For a biographical sketch of the artist, see Searles R. Boynton, D.D.S., *The Painter Lady, Grace Carpenter Hudson* (Eureka, Calif.: Interface California Corp., 1978). Biographical material on the artist is from this source.
2. Joseph Armstrong Baird, Jr., *Grace Carpenter Hudson (1865-1937),* exhibition catalog (San Francisco: California Historical Society, 1962), unpaginated.
3. Boynton, *Painter Lady,* 39-40.
4. Some of these reference photographs can be found in the Sun House, a repository for the artist's papers at Ukiah, California.
5. Boynton to Trenton, 2 March 1984. According to a native Pomoan, *Ka-ma* means "near the water" while the alternate title, *Found in the Brush,* is identified as a metaphor: "Father is unknown." Whether or not these sayings relate to biblical references, such as Moses in the bulrushes, is unclear. Grace Hudson's purpose in adopting this metaphor also is a mystery. In fact, we are told that many of Hudson's titles have a tendency to lean toward the bizarre when translated. We wish to express our gratitude to Suzanne Abel-Vidor, curator of the Sun House, Ukiah, California, who related this information to us.
6. Dr. Searles Boynton has informed Trenton that the models are identified in Grace Hudson's ledger at the Sun House.
7. This objective was expressed by the artist when she was asked to characterize her art: "My desire is that the world shall know them as I know them, and before they vanish . . . I must hurry to get the record complete before the opportunity is no more" (Suzanne Abel-Vidor, The Sun House, Sept., 1983).

Leigh   *Pool at Oraibi*

1. June DuBois, *W. R. Leigh: The Definitive Biography* (Kansas City: Lowell Press, 1977). See also Cummins, *William Robinson Leigh.* Both biographers give Leigh's birth date as 1866; the artist records it as 1863 in his autobiography, written some seventy years later.
2. William R. Leigh, "My Life," 2 vols. (Unpublished autobiography, Tulsa: Gilcrease Institute, Leigh Collection, n.d.). Other Leigh quotations are also from his autobiography.
3. See *Pool of Water on Acoma Rock. New Mexico,* Photography Files of William R. Leigh, Gilcrease Institute, Leigh Collection. We are grateful to Anne Morand, curator of art, Gilcrease Institute, who researched the Leigh Collection for us and brought the photograph to our attention.
4. Exhibition catalog, Gilcrease Institute, Leigh Collection.
5. Cummins, *William Robinson Leigh,* 135.
6. Ibid., 134.

Sharp   *Shelling Corn*

1. Forrest Fenn, *J. H. Sharp: The Beat of the Drum and the Whoop of the Dance* (Santa Fe: Fenn Publishing Co., 1983). This carefully researched book has a description by the artist of an earlier trip he took with Hauser through the Southwest in 1883 on which they reached Santa Fe but not Taos (Sharp to a correspondent, transcribed in Sharp's scrapbook, page 6; courtesy Fenn Galleries, Ltd., Archives, Sharp Collection, Santa Fe). We are deeply grateful

to Forrest Fenn for making these archival papers available to our researchers. See also Hauser entry in this catalog.

2. See Trenton introduction to *Picturesque Images from Taos and Santa Fe*, exhibition catalog (Denver: Denver Art Museum, 1974).

3. Robert R. White, ed., *The Taos Society of Artists* (Albuquerque: New Mexico University Press, 1983); prior to the publication of this book, the Taos Society Papers were stored in the basement of the Fine Arts Museum of New Mexico in Santa Fe where they were unindexed and unavailable to researchers. This probably explains the confusion over the date of the Society's founding, which was generally recorded as 1912.

4. For information on Sharp's studio and house, see the untitled newspaper clipping of November 1915 in Fenn Galleries, Ltd., Archives, Sharp Collection. We are indebted to Forrest Fenn for his willingness to share Sharp's papers with us.

5. According to current accounts, Phillips's Corn Husking series was shared by several of the Taos artists. Prints can also be found in the Sharp Collection. We are grateful to Curator Mary Cates, Blumenschein House, who brought the Phillips photographs to our attention.

Sharp *Crucita*

1. J. H. Sharp is quoted in "An Artist Among the Indians," *Brush and Pencil* 4 (April 1899): 7. The shawl illustrated is from Sharp's collection and was exhibited in the recent Sharp retrospective at the Fenn Galleries in November 1983.

2. See Fenn, *J. H. Sharp*, 318. Crucita's daughters Matilda Hadley and Nettie (Natividad) Lujan confirm that their mother stopped modeling when she married Jim Lucero in 1924. They believe that she was sixteen or seventeen when she posed for this painting.

3. "An Artist Among the Indians," 3.

Blumenschein *Old Man in White*

1. Trenton, *Picturesque Images*, 30.

2. Howard Cook, "Ernest L. Blumenschein," *New Mexico Quarterly Review* (Spring 1949): 20.

3. Trenton, *Picturesque Images*, 32, no. 20; 34, ill.

4. See n. 2 above.

5. Researcher Malin Wilson, Santa Fe, to Trenton, 19 January 1984. Most of her information about this Indian came from Tony Reyna (former regent of the University of New Mexico). The model appears in several of Blumenschein's paintings; see, for example, *The Medicine Man* in Ernest L. Blumenschein, "The Taos Society of Artists," *American Magazine of Art* 8 (September 1917): 451, ill.

6. The sketch for this painting is in the collection of Virginia Couse Leavitt, Tucson.

7. Blumenschein quoted in "Appreciation of Indian Art," *El Palacio* 6 (24 May 1919): 179.

8. A stone carved head belonging to Blumenschein is in the Blumenschein House, Kit Carson Memorial Foundation, Taos, New Mexico. The artist's daughter, Helen, related the following story to Curator Mary Cates, Blumenschein House. Helen and her father spotted the carved stone head on a wall outside of Santa Fe. They inquired if they could purchase it from the Hispanic owner and he agreed to sell it for five dollars. He told them it was a head from an Indian statue found in a canyon outside of Santa Fe. Neither Helen nor her father believed the story. They thought it might have been carved by its owner, and that it resembled the work of the carver Borella, or earlier Hispanic carvings of primitive origin. Despite its mysterious origins, the artist was quite taken with the stone head and explored its visual possibilities in several of his paintings, such as *The Plasterer* and *Jim Romero*; but, it was probably here in this earlier work of 1917 that he first adapted the image for a symbolic association with the model.

Blumenschein *Girl in Rose*

1. Blumenschein Papers, roll 269, frame 152, Archives of American Art, Smithsonian Institution, Washington, D.C. Our appreciation to Director Paul Karlstrom and his staff at the West Coast branch in San Francisco for the courtesy and assistance shown us.

2. See *El Palacio* 24 (23 June 1928): 492. Reprint of a review of the Blumenschein exhibition in Denver by artist Arnold Ronnebeck in the *Rocky Mountain News*.

3. Blumenschein quoted in William T. Henning, Jr., *Ernest L. Blumenschein/Retrospective* (Colorado Springs: Colorado Springs Fine Arts Center, 1978), 20.

4. Quoted from "Ernest L. Blumenschein: The Artist in His Environment," *New Mexico Quarterly Review* (Spring 1949), 18.

Berninghaus   *One of the Old Men of the Pueblo*

1. Laura M. Bickerstaff, *Pioneer Artists of Taos* (Denver: Sage Books, 1955), 8-9.
2. Van Deren Coke, *Taos and Santa Fe: The Artist's Environment, 1882-1942* (Albuquerque: New Mexico University Press, 1963). 18.
3. See Trenton, *Picturesque Images*, 18, no. 10; 21, ill.
4. Berninghaus to Dr. Carey B. Elliott, Taos, 14 January 1945. Courtesy of Forrest Fenn, Fenn Galleries, Ltd., Archives; and Berninghaus to R. L. Jameson, Fort Worth, 5 March 1940, Archives of American Art, Smithsonian Institution, Shuler-Berninghaus Collection, roll SW1, frame 314 (the latter a response about the painting *October—Taos* ["Indian with Pumpkin"]).
5. Quoted in Trenton, *Picturesque Images*, 20.
6. Coke, *Taos and Santa Fe*, 18.

Ufer   *Red Moccasins*

1. Ufer quoted in "Art in the Southwest," *El Palacio* 24 (19-26 May 1928): 403. We are grateful to Stephen Good of Rosenstock Arts, Denver, who brought this article and others about Ufer to our attention.
2. Ibid. 404.
3. Ibid.
4. Ufer quoted in "Paintings of the West," *El Palacio* 8 (July 1920): 242.
5. Ted and Kit Egri, "Walter Ufer: Passion and Talent," *American Artist* 24 (January 1978): 64.
6. *Walter Ufer: Sixteen Paintings, Christie's, Houston, October 16, 1982,* auction sales catalog foreword, unpaginated.

Higgins   *Daisy Mirabal*

1. Mabel Dodge Luhan, *Taos and Its Artists* (Duell, Sloan and Pearce: New York, 1947).
2. *Sleeping Nude* from this series, illustrated in *Art Digest* (15 February 1933): 10, demonstrates this fact by revealing the superstructure of diagonal and triangular lines. See Jay Hambidge, ed., "Dynamic Symmetry of the Human Figure for Advanced Students; Lesson II," *Diagonal* 1 (December 1919): 27-28.
3. For examples of Higgins's early work, see illustrations in the exhibition catalog by Dean Porter, *Victor Higgins, 1884-1949* (Indianapolis: Art Gallery, University of Notre Dame and Indianapolis Museum of Art, 1975), 9. A large European landscape by Higgins is in the collection of the Union League Club of Chicago.
4. Ibid., 14.
5. Higgins quoted in the *Santa Fe New Mexican*, 26 June 1940.
6. Higgins quoted by Ina Sizer Cassidy in "Art and Artists of New Mexico," *New Mexico Magazine* 2 (December 1932): 22.
7. Porter, *Victor Higgins*, 14.
8. Review of Higgins's exhibition at Chester Johnson Galleries, Chicago, in *El Palacio* 33 (7-14 December 1932): 224.
9. *The Santa Fe New Mexican*, 26 June 1940.

Adams   *Taos Indian*

1. Trenton, *Picturesque Images*, 6-11, and artist's biographical file, Museum of New Mexico Art Gallery, Santa Fe, information supplied by the artist in September 1960.
2. Lloyd Lózes Goff, "Kenneth M. Adams," *New Mexico Artists*, New Mexico Artists Series, no. 3 (Albuquerque: University of New Mexico Press, 1952), 54-55.
3. Ibid., 52.
4. There is a photograph of Adams holding the lithograph *Taos Indian* reproduced in an undated and unidentified newspaper, probably *Taos News*. The accompanying article mentions that the lithograph was among the works included in a 1964 Adams retrospective at the University of New Mexico Art Gallery, Albuquerque. It also states that the model was Joe Concha, a Taos Indian. A larger version of the lithograph, dated 1957, is listed in a 1972 sale at the Western Art Gallery in Albuquerque (no. 53). It appears that Adams may have

based this painting on two editions of the same lithographic subject. Yet a photograph of Concha taken about 1975, ten years after the painting was executed, shows him to be an old man. Thus it is unlikely that he posed as the young man in the painting just ten years earlier. If the model in the painting is actually Concha—and the features in painting and photograph do show some similarity—the work could have been based on an earlier sketch or on the artist's memory. The face in the painting, on the other hand, seems ageless and the artist may have idealized Concha's features. Joe Concha is alive and living in Taos, but his failing memory cannot provide the answer to this mystery. To add to the confusion, another Taos Indian, Louis Romero, has been suggested as the model, but he does not remember sitting for this picture either.

5. The incorrect placement of the blanket was pointed out to researcher Susan E. Nunemaker by Louis Romero of Taos. Nunemaker to Trenton, 31 January 1984.
6. Van Deren Coke, *Kenneth M. Adams: A Retrospective Exhibition* (Albuquerque: University of New Mexico, 1964), 11.
7. Ibid.

Couse *Blanket Seller*

1. Biographical information on the artist is from the following sources: Trenton, *Picturesque Images*, 54-58; Alta Edmondson, "E. Irving Couse, Painter of Indians," *Panhandle-Plains Historical Review* 42 (1969): 1-21; DeWitt Lockman, N.A., Interview with Couse, New York, 26 May 1927; conversations with Virginia Couse Leavitt, the artist's granddaughter, Tucson, who is preparing a book on Couse; and Rose Henderson, "A Painter of Pueblo Indians," *El Palacio* 10 (15 April 1921): 2-7.
2. Keith L. Bryant, Jr., *The Atchison, Topeka and Santa Fe Railway and the Development of the Taos and Santa Fe Art Colonies*, reprint, *Western Historical Quarterly* 9 (October 1978): 449.
3. See Trenton, *Picturesque Images*, 54.
4. DeWitt Lockman Interview; see M. Knoedler Galleries, New York, 18-28 February 1907, Couse exhibition catalog.
5. Virginia Couse to her sister Fan, Taos, 12 June 1902, L192:3, Couse Family Archives, Tucson. Couse's 1906 photographs of Big John Concha and another unidentified Indian in the Couse Family Archives show close physical resemblances to the model in this picture. We wish to thank Virginia Couse Leavitt and her family for their many courtesies and kindnesses.
6. Photographs in Couse Family Archives.
7. For a reproduction of *Moki Snake Dance*, Anschutz Collection, see Trenton, *Picturesque Images*, 55, no. 34.
8. Patricia Janis Broder, *Taos: A Painter's Dream* (Boston: New York Graphic Society, 1980), 140.

Sharp *Two Moons*

1. *El Palacio* 13 (1 September 1922): 67.
2. *Leslie Weekly*, 3 January 1907, courtesy of Fenn Galleries, Ltd., Archives, Sharp Collection.
3. Fenn, *J. H. Sharp*.
4. This is part of the inscription by the artist on the back of the canvas of the Los Angeles Athletic Club painting *Two Moons*.
5. A photograph of the Berkeley version is in the Sharp Photographic Collection, C. M. Russell Museum, Great Falls, Montana. Director Ray Steele kindly brought this to our attention.
6. Hamlin Garland, "General Custer's Last Fight as Seen by Two Moons," *McClure's Magazine* 11 (September 1898): 448.

Paxson *Little Bear*

1. "A Portfolio of the Art of E. S. Paxson . . ." *Montana Magazine of History* 4 (Spring 1954): 38.
2. Ibid., 31.
3. Edgar Samuel Paxson Journals (1898-99, 1901-19), Notes, and Studio Guest Registers in the Collection of William E. Paxson, Sr.
4. William E. Paxson, Jr., "E. S. Paxson: Frontier Artist," MS, VIII-3, to be published by Pruett

Publishing Co., Boulder, Colorado, in June 1984. We wish to express our appreciation to the Paxson family for sharing Paxson's memorabilia with us.

5. Ibid.

6. The latter is in the Los Angeles Athletic Club Collection.

7. The entry appears on a printed ledger form dated 1911, thereby causing some confusion about when the painting was actually finished; the date of "1912" inscribed on the work and the artist's recording of Vice President John S. Sherman's death in the same entry seem to confirm the later date. According to Paxson's account, he finished Little Bear's portrait on "October 31, 1911." There are, however, journal entries in which Paxson actually substituted the printed date for the correct one.

8. Mrs. Russell Palmer to the authors. See the frontispiece of Frank B. Linderman, *Indian Old-Man Stories* . . . (New York: Charles Scribner's Sons, 1920). We are grateful to Linderman's heirs for bringing this to our attention.

9. Frank Bird Linderman, *Montana Adventure*, edited by H. G. Merrian (Lincoln: University of Nebraska Press, 1968), 160. In a letter to Cato Sells, commissioner of Indian Affairs, 1 March 1916, Washington, D.C., Linderman elaborates on the plight of this small renegade band of Chippewa-Cree Indians and pleads to the United States government to establish a reservation for them. We are grateful to Linderman's heirs for providing a copy of the letter.

10. Linderman, *Montana Adventure*, 161.

Rollins *The Historian*

1. For biographical material on Rollins see Trenton, *Picturesque Images*, 178; Nancy Dustin Wall Moure and Lyn Wall Smith, *Dictionary of Art and Artists in Southern California Before 1930* (Los Angeles: Privately Printed, 1975), 213-14; and Marjorie Arkelian, *The Kahn Collection of Nineteenth-Century Paintings by Artists in California* (Oakland, Ca.: Oakland Museum Art Department, 1975), 43.

2. Warren Griffin, "A Circle of Light." (Unpublished biography, 1974), 64, deposited at New Mexico State Records Center and Archives, Santa Fe, Warren Griffin Collection. We wish to thank Archivist Sherry Smith-Gonzáles, for her assistance. Information about Rollins's travels in the Southwest is drawn from this source except where noted.

3. *The Santa Fe New Mexican*, 6 June 1910, p. 1.

4. Ibid.

5. Malin Wilson to Trenton, 22 February 1984. Polly Schaafsma, authority on rock art, related this information to Researcher Wilson.

6. *Los Angeles Times*, 25 September 1910, sec. 3, review by art critic Antony Anderson after visiting the artist in his studio.

7. *The Historian* was reproduced in the *Los Angeles Times*, 12 March, 1911, sec. 3, p. 18. In the accompanying article Antony Anderson announces Rollins's spring exhibition of desert and Indian pictures at Steckel Gallery and notes that the artist will devote the coming year to completing "his pictorial exposition of the life of the Indian, from pre-historic days to the present." He adds that "the artist has already won an enviable reputation for the fidelity he shows in his work among the red men, for his intelligent and sympathetic interpretation of their daily life, and for his appreciation of the deeper and more poetic aspects of their nature." Among the thirty-three paintings included in the exhibition, Anderson singles out *The Historian* for special praise and elaborates on it: "The tall, red-blanketed Indian in the picture is no decrepit savant bending over musty tomes. He is young and lithe and full of life. Instead of a pen he holds a graving tool, and he stands erect before a solid wall of sandstone, on which he is chiselling some romantic legend of his race—for he is a poet even more than he is a recorder of facts. The lines of his figure are severely simple and long, nobly sculpturesque in effect."

8. See n. 5 above.

9. Lovelace Medical Foundation Collection, Albuquerque, untitled and undated, the work measures 35⅝ × 24 inches.

10. Ramona Griffin, *Chaco Canyon Ruins* . . . , illustrated by Warren E. Rollins (Flagstaff, Ariz.: Northland Press, 1971).

11. Ina Sizer Cassidy, "Art and Artists of New Mexico," *New Mexico Magazine* (March 1948): 24 and 47.

12. Rollins quoted in Griffin, "A Circle of Light," 102-03.

Hauser *Wild Horse*

1. *Cyclopedia of Biography*, vol. 16, pp. 79-80. Courtesy Cincinnati Art Museum Library.
2. Fenn, *J. H. Sharp*, 49 ff.
3. From Sharp's scrapbook, Fenn Galleries, Ltd., Archives, Sharp Collection.
4. See n. 1 above.
5. Fenn, *J. H. Sharp*, 75.
6. See n. 1 above.

Raschen (1854-1937), *Pomo Interior*

Collections:
Julius Carlebach, New York; Museum of the American Indian, New York; Kennedy Galleries, New York, 1969 to 1973; Los Angeles Athletic Club, 1973.

Exhibitions:
Morris & Kennedy, San Francisco, 12 April 1884 (*The Argonaut*, 12 April 1884, p. 6).

A Plentiful Country: An Exhibition of Important Paintings of the American West, Kennedy Galleries, New York, June 1970; Knoedler Galleries, New York, 1971; Witte Memorial Museum, San Antonio, Tex., 1972. See "A Plentiful Country," *The Kennedy Quarterly* 10 (June 1970).

Hudson (1865-1937), *Ka-ma-ko-ya*

Collections:
Wolf & John Pogzeba, Denver, 1965; Steve Rose, Biltmore Galleries, Los Angeles, 1965; Los Angeles Athletic Club, 1969.

Exhibition:
Pogzeba Exhibition, The Old Church, Denver, 1965.

Leigh (1866-1955), *Pool at Oraibi*

Collections:
Jamison Gallery, Santa Fe; Sotheby Parke-Bernet, New York; Los Angeles Athletic Club, 1973.

Exhibitions:
Babcock Art Galleries, 1918.

The West as Art, Palm Springs Desert Museum, 24 February-30 March 1982, catalog essay by Patricia Trenton.

Sharp (1859-1953), *Shelling Corn*

Collections:
John J. Kirk from artist, Sharp's sales ledger, Gallup, N.M., August, 1945; Kirk descendants by inheritance, Santa Fe, ca. 1950; Fenn Galleries, Ltd., Santa Fe, 1976; Robert J. Dunn, M.D., Mesa, Ariz., 1976-78; Fenn Galleries, Ltd., 1978; Morrie Zinman, Blue Bell, Pa., 1978-82; Gerald P. Peters Gallery, Santa Fe, 1982; Los Angeles Athletic Club, 1982.

Exhibitions:
Exhibition of/Indian Paintings/by J. H. Sharp/at/ The Traxel Art Galleries/ . . . November 23rd to December 5/1925/Cincinnati, Ohio, exhibition catalog, no. 25.

. . . J. H. Sharp/ . . . Exhibitions of/Indian and Other Paintings/at the/ Traxel Art Galleries/ . . . /November 28th to December 10th/ Cincinnati, Ohio/1927, exhibition catalog, no. 30.,

American Federation of Arts, summer 1929. *American Magazine of Art* 20 (July 1929); 419, ill.

J. H. Sharp: The Beat of the Drum and the Whoop of the Dance, Fenn Galleries, Santa Fe, November 1938.

Sharp, *Crucita*

Collections:
Cowie Galleries from artist, Los Angeles; Biltmore Galleries, Los Angeles; George Landes, Monrovia, Ca.; Biltmore Galleries; Forrest Fenn Collection, Santa Fe, 1974; Los Angeles Athletic Club, 1983.

Exhibitions:
Since there are so many versions of *Crucita—Taos Indian Girl* (and no dimensions given in the several exhibition catalogs that list this title), and because the Los Angeles Athletic Club picture has a known history in California collections, I have chosen to list only shows that took place in California galleries and one in Hawaii after the recorded date of this painting ("1924" by Sharp

on the canvas back), which appears to be the latest version; the first was noted about 1915.

Exhibition of/ Indian Paintings/by/ . . . J. H. Sharp/ . . . /at/ Grace Nicholson's Galleries/ . . . /March tenth to April tenth/ Pasadena/ 1925, exhibition catalog, no. 1.

. . . J. H. Sharp/ . . . Indian Paintings/at/The Schroeder Galleries/ . . . Feb. 1st to Feb. 13th/Pasadena/1927, exhibition catalog, no. 22.

California Palace of the Legion of Honor, San Francisco, 1928, recorded in *El Palacio* 25 (24 November 1928): 361.

. . . J. H. Sharp/ . . . Hawaiian and Taos Paintings/at Gump's Fine Art Gallery/Honolulu, 1931, exhibition catalog, no. 6.

Blumenschein (1874-1960), *Old Man in White*

Collections:
Grand Central Galleries, New York, 1961; Robert Rockwell, Corning, N.Y., October 1961; Rosenstock Arts, Denver; Fenn Galleries, Ltd., Santa Fe; Wilfred Friedman, M.D., Santa Fe; Gerald P. Peters, Santa Fe; Los Angeles Athletic Club, 1982.

Exhibition:
Grand Central Galleries, New York, 1961.

Blumenschein, *Girl in Rose*

Collections:
Grand Central Galleries, New York, 1927; Schweitzer Gallery, New York, 1963; Jamison Gallery, Santa Fe, 1964; William Griffith, Santa Fe & Dallas, 1966; Hall Galleries, Fort Worth, 1982; William C. Foxley, Denver, 1982; Rosenstock Arts, Denver, 1983; Los Angeles Athletic Club, 1984.

Exhibition:
Grand Central Galleries, New York, 4-23 February 1927, no. 9 (Blumenschein Papers, see n.1).

Berninghaus (1874-1952), *One of the Old Men*

Collections:
Robert E. Evelyn McKee from artist, El Paso, Tex., ca. 1935; Louis McKee by inheritance; Gerald P. Peters, Santa Fe; Los Angeles Athletic Club, 1982.

Exhibitions:
Catalogue of the 122nd Annual Exhibition, January 30, to March 20, 1927, The Pennsylvania Academy of the Fine Arts, Philadelphia, 30, no. 103, ill.

Catalogue of the Fortieth Annual Exhibition of American Paintings and Sculpture/ The Art Institute of Chicago/ October 27, to December 14, 1927, no. 17. Des Moines Association of Fine Arts; Nebraska Art Association, Lincoln; Kansas City Art Institution, 6 January-29 April 1928 (Berninghaus Correspondence, Shuler-Berninghaus Collection, Archives of American Art, Smithsonian Institution, roll SWI, frame 314.)

The McKee Collection of Paintings, El Paso Museum of Art, 3-24 November 1968, exhibition catalog, no. 18.

Ufer (1876-1936), *Red Moccasins*

Collections:
John A. Ware from artist, Chicago, 1917; Morrie Zinman, New Bell, Pa., Gerald P. Peters, Santa Fe, 1983; Los Angeles Athletic Club, 1983.

Higgins (1884-1949), *Daisy Mirabal*

Collections:
Joan Higgins Reed, the artist's daughter, by inheritance: Jamison Gallery, Santa Fe, 1966; William Griffith, Dallas, Tex., 1966-81; Ron Hall Galleries, Fort Worth, 1981; Ken C. Martin, New

Orleans, 1981; Ron Hall Galleries, 1982; Gerald P. Peters, Santa Fe, 1982; Los Angeles Athletic Club, 1982.

Exhibitions:
Chester Johnson Galleries, Chicago, December 1932.

Victor Higgins Memorial Exhibition, Museum of New Mexico Art Gallery, Santa Fe, 3-24 February 1957, exhibition catalog, no. 23.

Adams (1897-1966), *Taos Indian*

Collections:
Jamison Gallery, Santa Fe, 1965; William Griffith, Dallas and Santa Fe, 1966-82; Hall Galleries, Fort Worth, 1982; William C. Foxley, Denver, 1982; Gerald P. Peters, Santa Fe; Los Angeles Athletic Club, 1982.

Exhibition:
. . . an exhibition of the oil paintings of Kenneth M. Adams, N.A., Jamison Gallery, Santa Fe, 15 October-1 November 1965, exhibition catalog, no. 6.

Couse (1866-1936), *Blanket Seller*

Collections:
Mr. and Mrs. Charles D. Owen, Jr., New Canaan, Conn., 1969; M. Knoedler Galleries, New York, 1970; Berry-Hill Galleries, Inc., New York, 1972-73; Morrie Zinman, Blue Bell, Pa.; Gerald P. Peters, Santa Fe, 1982; Los Angeles Athletic Club, 1982.

Exhibition:
Cowboys, Indians, Trappers and Traders, Amherst College, Amherst, Mass., 1-28 February 1973, exhibition catalog.

Sharp, *Two Moons*

Collections:
King C. Gillette, Brookline, Mass., Sharp's sales ledger, March 1911; private collection, San Francisco; Fenn Galleries, Ltd., Santa Fe, 1982; Los Angeles Athletic Club, 1983.

Exhibitions:
Pictures of the West by J. H. Sharp at the Closson Galleries, Cincinnati [1911], exhibition catalog, no. 14.

J. H. Sharp: The Beat of the Drum and the Whoop of the Dance, Fenn Galleries, Ltd., Santa Fe, November 1983, exhibition brochure, no. 10.

Paxson (1852-1919), *Little Bear*

Collections:
John Ritch from artist, Lewistown, Mont.; Ritch's daughter, Mrs. Russell Palmer, by inheritance; Biltmore Galleries, Los Angeles; Los Angeles Athletic Club, 1980.

Rollins (1861-1962), *The Historian*

Collections:
Henry Lewis, Lubbock, Tex.; Gerald P. Peters, Santa Fe, 1979; Los Angeles Athletic Club, 1979.

Exhibitions:
Warren E. Rollins, Desert and Indian Pictures, Steckel Gallery, Los Angeles, 10-24 March 1911.

The West as Art, Palm Springs Desert Museum, 24 February-30 March 1982, catalog essay by Patricia Trenton.

Hauser (1859-1913), *Wild Horse*

Collections:
F. Bardes from artist, Cincinnati; Kodner Galleries, Saint Louis; Terry DeLapp, Los Angeles; Los Angeles Athletic Club, 1982.

Composed in Garamond Light by Type Works, Pasadena. Printed on Lustro
Offset Enamel Dull by Typecraft, Inc., Pasadena.